SOURCES ᵣ ᵤₖ IRISH GENEALOGY IN THE LIBRARY OF THE SOCIETY OF GENEALOGISTS

Compiled by
Anthony J. Camp

Published by the Society of Genealogists

Published by
Society of Genealogists
14 Charterhouse Buildings
Goswell Road
London EC1M 7BA

Registered Charity No. 233701

First published 1990
Second edition 1998

ISBN 1 85951 501 0

CONTENTS

INTRODUCTION

Although not extensive the collection of Irish material at the Society of Genealogists provides a group of basic works which is easily accessible in central London.

The Library was founded in 1911. Although its greatest value is undoubtedly for the seeker after English ancestry, the Society has always been interested in collecting data on families anywhere in the British Isles and their connections overseas. There are thus basic collections for all the countries of the former Empire and Commonwealth and some material, including genealogical periodicals, from most countries worldwide.

The general collections have expanded rapidly in recent years and are briefly described in the outline *Using the library of the Society of Genealogists*, which is revised and re-printed regularly.

Catalogues of several sections of the Library have also been published and are in print: Parish Register copies, Monumental Inscriptions, Directories and Poll Books, Census Indexes, Will Indexes and other Probate Material, and School and University Registers. All these list relevant Irish material in those categories but additional material is continually being received. Catalogues of the Scottish and East Indian material have also been published.

The material relating directly to Ireland is conveniently situated on the 'Irish Shelves' in the Middle Library, but information on Irish families may be found elsewhere, particularly in the Document Collection and in the collection of Family Histories. Any name should thus always be checked in the card catalogue of Family Histories, in the Document Collection (which is self-indexing), and in the Index of Pedigrees in Special Collections.

The bibliographies of printed Irish family histories and pedigrees, *Bibliography of Irish genealogy and family history*, by Brian de Breffny (1964) and *Bibliography of Irish family history* by Edward MacLysaght (1982) will lead to pedigrees in a wide variety of sources, including periodicals. Both should be consulted. They include references to pedigrees in such works as Burke's *Landed gentry of Ireland*, Howard and Crisp's *Visitation of Ireland*, O'Hart's *Irish pedigrees* and Archdall's *Lodge's Peerage of Ireland*.

The arrangement of the material on the Irish Shelves follows that of the Library Catalogue, the whole of Ireland (Northern Ireland and Eire) being divided into seven sections: General (including Wills) **[IR/GEN]**, Local **[IR/LOC]**, Registers **[IR/R]**, Monumental Inscriptions **[IR/M]**, Censuses **[IR/C]**, Lists **[IR/D]**, and Periodicals **[IR/PER]**.

This book, for ease of reference, rearranges the material by county. Each county section is divided into eight subjects: (1) **CENSUSES**, by date; (2) **LISTS AND DIRECTORIES**, by date; (3) **LOCAL HISTORY**, by parish, prefaced with **Maps** and material covering the whole **County**; (4) **MONUMENTAL INSCRIPTIONS**, by parish; (5) **NEWSPAPERS**; (6) **PARISH REGISTERS**, by parish; (7) **PERIODICALS**; and (8) **SCHOOLS**, by place.

Prior to the sections by county there is a **GENERAL** section of works which cover the whole or large areas of Ireland, arranged by subject in alphabetical order, from **Architects** to **Workhouses**. The standard guides to research in Ireland are listed there under **Research**. This is followed by sections on **PARISH AND NONCONFORMIST REGISTERS** dealing with **General guides** and **Composite indexes**, **MARRIAGE LICENCES** arranged by diocese, **MONUMENTAL INSCRIPTIONS, LISTS AND DIRECTORIES WITH NATIONAL COVERAGE, PERIODICALS**, and on **WILLS** arranged by diocese and including **Other testamentary material.**

All the Irish material held by the Society is listed here, including accessions reported in the March 1998 issue of the *Genealogists' Magazine*. For ease of reference within the library shelf references have been added in each case. The book developed from an article first contributed to *North Irish Roots* (1989) which was expanded into a lecture, 'Sources for Irish genealogy at the Society of Genealogists', delivered at the 1st Irish Genealogical Congress at Dublin in 1991 and published in *Aspects of Irish genealogy* (1993) **[IR/G 194].**

ABBREVIATIONS

B	Burials
C	Christenings
D	Deaths
M	Marriages
MF	Microfilm
Mfc	Microfiche
PRONI	Public Record Office of Northern Ireland
RC	Roman Catholic
TS	Typescript

GENERAL

Archaeology: *The archaeology of medieval Ireland*, by T.B. Barry (London, 1987) **[IR/G 146]**

Architects: *A biographical dictionary of architects in Ireland 1600-1720*, by R. Loeber (1981) **[IR/G 204]**

Architecture: *Classical churches in Ulster*, by J.S. Curl (Belfast, 1980) **[IR/L 151]**. *Introduction to Ulster architecture*, by H. Dixon (Belfast, 1975) **[IR/L 152]**. *Ulster architecture 1800-1900: an exhibition of architectural drawings with photographs & portraits*, by H. Dixon (Belfast, 1972) **[Ireland Tracts 1]**

Archives *see* **Public Records**

Army: *History of the Irish army*, by J.P. Duggan (Dublin, 1991) **[IR/G 177]**. *Illustrations, historical and genealogical of King James's Irish army list 1689*, by J. D'Alton (2 vols., Dublin, n.d.) **[IR/G 68-9]**. *History of the Irish brigades in the service of France 1688-1789*, by J.C. O'Callaghan (Glasgow, 1886) **[ARM/GEN 34]**. *Ireland's memorial records 1914-1918, being the names of Irishmen who fell in the Great European War* (Committee of the Irish National War Memorial, 8 vols., Dublin, 1923) **[Irish Folio Shelves]**. *The Royal Irish Fusiliers 1793-1950*, by M. Cunliffe (London, 1952) **[ARM/RH 83]**. *The story of the Fifth Royal Inniskilling Dragoon Guards*, by R. Evans (Aldershot, 1951) **[ARM/RH 30]**. *The Inniskilling Dragoons: the records of an old heavy cavalry regiment*, by E.S. Jackson (London, 1909) **[ARM/RH 3]**. *With the Inniskilling Dragoons: the record of a cavalry regiment during the Boer War, 1899-1902*, by J.W. Yardley (London, 1904) **[ARM/RH 31]**. *The regimental records of the First Battalion the Royal Dublin Fusiliers 1644-1842* (London, 1910) **[ARM/RH 96]**. *London Irish Rifles 1859-1959*, by Lt.Col. Corbally (1959) **[ARM/RH 94]**. 'Regiments disbanded in Ireland 1698', in *Some Irish lists*, vol. 2 **[IR/G 124]**. 'Military officers of the Irish establishment in 1736', in *Some Irish lists*, vol. 2 **[IR/G 124]**. 'Officers of the Irish Volunteers 1782', in *Some Irish lists*, vol. 1 **[IR/G 123]**. 'Yeomanry officers of Ireland 1796', in *Some Irish lists*, vol. 1 **[IR/G 123]**. 'Some officers of the Irish militia 1793', in *Some Irish lists*, vol. 2 **[IR/G 124]**. 'Field officers of the Irish militia 1803', in *Some Irish lists*, vol. 2 **[IR/G 124]**. 'Officers of the Irish militia 1804-1809', in *Some Irish lists*, vol. 2 **[IR/G 124]**. 'Records of the Irish in the British army', by S. Colwell, in *Aspects of Irish genealogy* (1993) **[IR/G 194]**

Associations: *Directory of British associations & associations in Ireland*, Edition 11 **[Enquiry desk]**. *Yearbook of scientific & learned societies of Great Britain & Ireland, 1884* (1885) **[PR/SCI]**

Bibliography: *Subject matter catalogue of the library of the Irish Genealogical Research Society* (TS, 1965) **[IR/G 187]**. *Bibliography of Irish genealogy and family history*, by B. de Breffny (Cork & Dublin, 1964) **[Enquiry Desk, Shelf 8]**. *Bibliography of Irish family history*, by E. MacLysaght (Blackrock, 1982) **[Enquiry Desk, Shelf 8]**. *The history of the Irish in Britain: a bibliography*, by M. Hartigan (London, 1986) **[IR/G 162]**. *Ireland: the Albert E. Casey collection and other Irish materials in the Samford University Library; an annotated bibliography*, ed. G.V. Fleming-Haigh (Birmingham, Alabama, 1976) **[IR/G 27]**. *Additional Irish materials in the Samford University Library: a supplement to Fleming-Haigh's bibliography of the Albert E. Casey collection*, by M.M. Morton (Samford, 1985) **[IR/G 28]**. *Irish holdings of the Society of Australian Genealogists in the overseas library and primary records collection*, by H. Garnsey et al. (1996) **[IR/G 218]**. *A consolidated* index to the records of the Genealogical Office, Dublin, Ireland, vols. 1 A-C, 2 D-H, 3 I-O, 4 P-Z, by V.W. McAnlis (Port Angeles, 1994-7) **[IR/G 214]**

Biography: Lives of illustrious and distinguished Irishmen, by J Wills (vols. 1-2, 3 Part 1, 4 Part 2, Dublin, 1840-3) **[IR/G 7-12]**. The Irish nation: its history & its biography, by J & F Wills (4 vols., Edinburgh, 1875) **[IR/G 54-7]**. Index to persons in Lewis's Topographical dictionary of Ireland 1846, by F Wall (TS, n.d.) **[IR/G 2]**. A compendium of Irish biography, by A Webb (Dublin, 1878) **[IR/G 6]**. Biographical dictionary of Irishmen in France, by RHayes (Dublin, 1949) **[IR/G 3]**. A concise dictionary of Irish biography, by J S Crone (Liechtenstein, 1970) **[IR/G 5]**. A dictionary of Irish biography, by J Boyland (Dublin, 1978) **[IR/G 4]**. A biographical dictionary of Irish writers, by A M Brady & B Cleeve (Westmeath, 1985) **[IR/G 148]**

Body snatchers: The Irish body snatchers: a history of body snatching in Ireland, by J. Fleetwood (1988) **[IR/G 212]**

Censuses: A census of Ireland circa 1659 with supplementary material from the poll money ordinances 1660-1661 by S Pender (Dublin, Irish Manuscripts Commission, 1939) **[IR/G 135]**. General alphabetical index to the townlands and towns, parishes and baronies of Ireland 1851 (1861, reprinted 1984). Abstract of the census of the United Kingdom of Great Britain & Ireland 1861 [index of place names] **[TB/GAZ]**. Alphabetical index to the townlands and towns of Ireland for the census of Ireland 1871 (Dublin, 1877) **[IR/C 1]**. 1766 religious census of Ireland [survey of surviving originals and transcripts], by M T Medlycott (TS, 1992) **[IR/G 182]**. For individual censuses of counties and parishes see the **CENSUS** sections under **COUNTIES** below

Civil Survey 1654-6: The Civil Survey 1654-1656, vol. 10, Miscellanea ed. R C Simington (Dublin, 1961) **[IR/G 24]**. For individual county volumes see the **LOCAL** sections under **COUNTIES** below.

Clergy: An account of the ecclesiastical establishment subsisting in Ireland, ed. J C Erck (Dublin, 1830; incomplete copy) **[IR/G 25]**. Index to the names occuring in the extracts relating to advowsons of churches in Ireland appended to J F Ferguson's remarks on the Limitation of Actions Bill 1843, by G S Cary (TS, 1935) **[IR/G 122]**. The Irish church directory and year book 1932 ed. J B Leslie (Dublin, 1932) **[IR/G 26]**. Ardfert and Aghadoe clergy and parishes, by J B Leslie (Dublin, 1940) **[IR/L 8]**. Armagh clergy and parishes, by J B Leslie (Dundalk, 1911) **[IR/L 9]**. Clogher clergy and parishes, by J B Leslie (Enniskillen, 1929) **[IR/L 20]**. Clergy of Connor from patrician times to the present day, based on the unpublished succession lists compiled by Canon J B Leslie (1993) **[IR/G 185]**. Clerical and parochial records of Cork, Cloyne and Ross, by W M Brady (3 vols., Dublin, 1863-4) **[IR/L 23-5]**. Clerical and parochial records in the Diocese of Cork, Cloyne and Ross with genealogical and biographical data [1291-1860], by W M Brady (TS, vols. 2 & 3, 1963) **[IR/G 196]**. Derry clergy and parishes, by J B Leslie (Enniskillen, 1937) **[IR/L 27]**. 'Derry clergy', in Some Irish lists, vol. 4 **[IR/G 126]**. Biographical succession lists of the clergy of Down, by J B Leslie & H B Swanzy (Enniskillen, 1936) **[IR/L 34]**. Succession lists of the clergy of Dromore, by H B Swanzy (Belfast, 1933) **[IR/L 36]**. 'Ordinations and appointments to curacies & livings, dioceses of Dublin and Meath', in Some Irish lists, vol. 7 **[IR/G 129]**. Ferns clergy and parishes, by J B Leslie (Dublin, 1936) **[IR/L 45]**. 'Extracts from Ferns diocesan registers', in Some Irish lists, vol. 4 **[IR/G 126]**. 'Killaloe clergy in 1612', in Some Irish lists, vol. 7 **[IR/G 129]**. Ossory clergy and parishes, by J B Leslie (Enniskillen, 1933)

2

[IR/L 72]. 'Ulster ministers under the Commonwealth', in *Some Irish lists*, vol. 2 [IR/G 124]

Convert Rolls: *The Convert Rolls*, by E. O'Byrne (Dublin, 1981) [IR/G 156]

Coroners *see* **Officials**

Country Houses: *Burke's guide to country houses, vol. 1, Ireland*, by M Bence-Jones (London, 1978) [TB/TOP]. *Noble dwellings of Ireland*, by J F Mills (New York, 1978) [IR/G 168]

Deeds and manuscripts: *The Hamilton manuscripts: containing some account of the settlement of the territories of the Upper Clandeboye, Great Ardes, and Dufferin, in the County of Down, by Sir James Hamilton, Knight*, ed. T K Lowry (Belfast, 1867) [IR/G 30]. *Dowdall deeds*, ed. C McNeill & A J Otway-Ruthven (Dublin, 1960) [IR/G 31]. *The Inchiquin manuscripts*, ed. J Ainsworth (Dublin, 1961) [IR/G 32]. *The Kenmare manuscripts*, ed. E MacLysaght (Dublin, 1942) [IR/G 33]. *Calendar of Orrery papers*, ed. E MacLysaght (Dublin, 1941) [IR/G 34]. *An Anglo-Irish dialogue: a calendar of the correspondence between John Foster and Lord Sheffield 1774-1821* (PRONI, c.1981) [IR/G 44]. *Irish monastic and episcopal deeds, AD.1200-1600*, ed. N B White (Dublin, 1936) [IR/G 7⁴]

Education *see* **Schools**

Emigration: general: 'Irish Jacobites', by J G Simms, in *Analecta Hibernica*, vol. 22 (1960) 11-230 [IR/PER]. 'State-aided emigration schemes from crown estates in Ireland c.1850', by E Ellis, in *Analecta Hibernica*, vol. 22 (1960) 329-407 [IR/PER]. *Irish emigration lists 1833-1839 ... extracted from the Ordnance Survey memoirs for ... Londonderry and Antrim*, by B Mitchell (Baltimore, 1989) [IR/G 158]. *Ireland and Irish emigration to the New World from 1815 to the Famine* [IR/G 183]. *Irish research: the 1840's famine and its effects on emigration* [Audio cassette]

Emigration: America: *Ulster emigration to colonial America 1718-1775*, by R.J. Dickson (London, 1966) [US/MIG]. *Immigration of the Irish quakers into Pennsylvania 1682-1750*, by A.C. Myers (1902, reprinted Baltimore, 1985) [US/PA/G 10]. *Scotch-Irish migration to South Carolina 1772*, by J. Stephenson (1971) [US/SC/G 1]. *The famine immigrants: lists of [651,931] Irish immigrants arriving at the port of New York 1846-1851* ed. I.A. Glazier & M. Tepper (7 vols., Baltimore, 1983-86) [US/MIG 3-9]. *Irish passenger lists 1847-1871: lists of passengers sailing from Londonderry to America*, by B. Mitchell (Baltimore, 1988) [IR/G 153]. *The search for missing friends: Irish immigrant advertisements placed in the Boston Pilot*, vol. 1 1831-50 [US/MIG 69], vol. 2 1851-3 [US/MIG 70], vol. 3 1854-6 [US/MIG 71], vol. 4 1857-60 [US/MIG 71A]. *Irish passenger lists 1803-06: lists of passengers sailing from Ireland to America extracted from the Hardwicke Papers* [US/MIG 89]. *Lists of some passengers to the United States of America from England and Ireland 1841-60* [US/MIG 85]. *A history of the Irish settlers in North America, from the earliest period to the census of 1850* [US/MIG 81]. *Emigrants from Ireland to America 1735-43: a transcription of the Report of the Irish House of Commons into enforced emigration to America* [US/MIG 76]. *Irish American voluntary organizations*, by M F Funchion (1983) [US/G 150]. 'U.S. sources for Irish genealogy', by M E Daly, in *Aspects of Irish genealogy* (1993) [IR/G 194]

Emigration: Australia and New Zealand: *Irish families in Australia and New Zealand 1788-1981*, by H W Coffey & M J Morgan, 1st ed. vols. 3 (L-Q) and 4 (R-Z) (1980) and 2nd ed. vol. 2 (E-L) (1985) only [all AUA/G 28]. *The Irish Australians: selected articles for Australians and Irish family historians* [AUA/G 112].

'Australian sources to help Irish genealogy', by J Harrison, in *Aspects of Irish genealogy* (1993) **[IR/G 194]**

Emigration: Canada: *'Missing persons' from Ireland: notices from newspapers of St John, New Brunswick 1828-1906*, by C Addington (London, Ontario, 1987) **[IR/G 140]**. *Lists of some passengers: ... Ireland to Canada* **[CAN/G 57]**. *Irish emigrants' letters from Canada 1839-70* **[CAN/G 75]**. *Flight from famine: the coming of the Irish to Canada* **[CAN/G 76]**. 'Canadian sources for Irish genealogy', by B. Elliott, in *Aspects of Irish genealogy* (1993) **[IR/G 194]**

Emigration: England: *The history of the Irish in Britain: a bibliography*, by M Hartigan (London, 1986) **[IR/G 162]**

Emigration: France: *History of the Irish brigades in the service of France 1688-1789*, by J C O'Callaghan (Glasgow, 1886) **[ARM/GEN 34]**. *Biographical dictionary of Irishmen in France*, by R Hayes (Dublin, 1949) **[IR/G 3]**. *The Irish chateaux: in search of the Wild Geese*, by R Holohan (Dublin, 1989) **[IR/G 159]**

Emigration: India: 'Sources for Irish genealogy in the India Office Records', by T. Thomas, in *Aspects of Irish genealogy* (1993) **[IR/G 194]**

Emigration: New Zealand *see* **Australia**

Emigration: Scotland: *Irish-born secular priests in Scotland 1829-1979*, by B.J. Canning (Inverness, 1979) **[SC/G 199]**

Emigration: South America: 'The Irish in South America', by G. MacLoughlin, in *Aspects of Irish genealogy* (1993) **[IR/G 194]**

Emigration: Spain: *Spanish knights of Irish origin: documents from continental archives*, ed. M. Walsh (3 vols., Dublin, 1960, 1965, 1970) **[P/R/SPA]**

Emigration: Wales: *Little Ireland: aspects of the Irish and Greenhill, Swansea*, by R.T. Price (Swansea, 1992) **[WS/L 80]**

Estate towns: 'New sources for the history of estate towns in eighteenth and nineteenth century Ireland', by S.E. Hood, in *Aspects of Irish genealogy* (1993) **[IR/G 194]**

Famine: *The great Irish famine: words and images from the Famine Museum, Strokestown Park, County Roscommon*, by S.J. Campbell (1994) **[IR/G 215]**. *This great calamity: the Irish famine 1845-52*, by C. Kinealy (1994) **[IR/G 199]**. *Irish research: the 1840's famine and its effect on emigration*, by K. Whelan **[Audio cassette, 1995]**

Freemen: 'Sources for Irish freemen', by M. Clark, in *Aspects of Irish genealogy* (1993) **[IR/G 194]**

Friends *see* **Quakers**

Gazetteer *see* **Maps**

Genealogical Office: *A consolidated index to the records of the Genealogical Office, Dublin, Ireland, vols. 1 A-C, 2 D-H, 3 I-O, 4 P-Z*, by V.W. McAnlis (Port Angeles, 1994-7) **[IR/G 214]**. *See also* **Heraldry**

Griffith's Valuation and Tithe Applotment Books 1844-60: Index of Surnames (Mfc, 1982) **[Apply to staff]**. *Griffith's valuation: a vital link in Irish research*, by S McVetty **[Audio cassette, 1995]**. For individual county indexes and transcripts *see* the **COUNTIES** section below

Health: *White plague in Ulster: a short history of tuberculosis in Northern Ireland*, by H G Calwell & D H Craig (Belfast, n.d.) **[IR/G 173]**. *See also* **Body Snatchers** above, and **Hospitals**, **Nurses**, **Surgeons** and **Workhouses** below

Heraldry: *A catalogue of autograph letters addressed to Sir William Betham, Ulster King of Arms, 1810-1830*, by G F T Sherwood (London, 1936, with TS index) **[IR/G 13]**; another copy without index **[Ireland Tracts 1]**. *A consolidated index to the records of the Genealogical Office, Dublin, Ireland, vols. 1 A-C,*

2 D-H, 3 I-O, 4 P-Z, by V W McAnlis (Port Angeles, 1994-7) **[IR/G 214]**. 'Arms of Irish bishops from the Reformation to 1888', in *Some Irish lists*, vol. 3 **[IR/G 125]**. *Kennedy's book of arms*, by P. Kennedy (1816, reprinted 1967) **[IR/G 221]**. *Hatchments in Britain, vol. 10, The development and use of hatchments together with the hatchments of Ireland ...*, by T E Titterton (1994) **[HER/ARM]**. General works such as *The general armory of England, Scotland, Ireland and Wales*, by Sir J.B. Burke (1884); *Papworth's ordinary of British armorials* (1874) and *Fairbairn's book of crests of the families of Great Britain and Ireland* (1905) are found on the **Heraldry Shelves**. *See also* **Pedigrees**, **Peerage** and **Surnames** below.

High Sheriffs *see* **Officials**

History: *Description of Ireland and the state thereof ... 1598*, by E. Hogan (Dublin, 1878) **[IR/G 47]**. *A concise view of the origin ... of the new plantation in Ulster ... called the Irish Society* (London, 1842) **[IR/G 45]**. *The Cromwellian settlement of Ireland*, by J.P. Prendergast (London, 1870) **[IR/G 46]**. *The general history of Ireland*, by J. Keating (n.p., n.d.) **[IR/G 48]**. *The history of Ireland, by the Abbe MacGeoghegan* continued, by J. Mitchel (n.d.) **[IR/G 49]**. *The history of Ireland, ancient and modern*, by J. Mitchel (New York, n.d.) **[IR/G 50]**. *Ireland in the 17th century or the Irish massacres of 1641-2 their causes & results*, by M. Hickson (2 vols., London, 1884) **[IR/G 52-3]**, with TS index, by P. Manning (1990) **[IR/G 53A]**). *Advertisements for Ireland: being a description of the state of Ireland in the reign of James I*, ed. G. O'Brien (Dublin, 1923) **[IR/G 119]**. *The ancient land tenures of Ireland*, by D. Coghlan (Dublin, 1933) **[IR/G 64]**. *The old English in Ireland 1625-42*, by A. Clarke (Worcester & London, 1966) **[IR/G 58]**. *Intermarriage in Ireland 1550-1650*, by D. Jackson (Montreal, 1970) **[IR/G 144]**. *Ascendancy to oblivion: the story of the Anglo-Irish*, by M. McConville (London, 1986) **[IR/G 37]**. *A short history of Ireland*, by J.C. Beckett (London, 1986) **[IR/G 161]**. 'Calendar of the Irish Council Book 1581-6 by J.P. Prendergast', ed. D.B. Quinn, in *Analecta Hibernica*, No. 24 (Irish Manuscripts Commission, 1967) **[IR/PER]**. *The Irish administration 1801-1914*, by R.B. McDowell (1964, reprinted 1976) **[IR/G 193]**. *The Norman invasion of Ireland*, by R. Roche (2nd edn. 1995) **[IR/G 198]**. *Memoirs of the different rebellions in Ireland from the arrival of the English: also a particular detail of that which broke out the 23rd of May, 1798; with the history of the conspiracy which preceded it*, by R. Musgrave (4th edn. ed. S.W. Myers & D.E. McKnight, 1995) **[IR/G 137]**. *The 1798 rebellion in Ireland and its records*, by K. Whelan (1991) **[Audio cassette]**

Hospitals: *The hospitals and health services yearbook 1985: & directory of hospital suppliers: an annual record of the hospitals and health services of Great Britain & Northern Ireland, incorporating 'Burdett's Hospitals & Charities', founded 1889* (1985) **[PR/HEA]**. *See also* **Workhouses** below

Huguenots: *The Huguenots, their settlements, churches and industries in England and Ireland*, by S. Smiles (London, 1876) **[HUG/GEN]**. *The French settlers in Ireland: the settlements in Waterford*, by T. Gimlette (Waterford, 1856) **[IR/G 51]**. *History of the Huguenot settlers in Ireland*, by T. Gimlette (Dunmore East, 1888) **[IR/G 51]**. 'The Huguenots in Ulster', by R.A. McCall, reprinted from *Proceedings of the Huguenot Society of London*, vol. 10 (London, 1915), no. 3 **[Ireland Tracts 1]**. *The Huguenots and Ireland: anatomy of an emigration*, by C.E.J. Caldicott et al. (1987) **[IR/G 217]**. *Anatomy of the Huguenot migration to Ireland*, by R. Vigne (1994) **[Audio cassette]**. *See also* **Immigration** below and for the registers of the French churches at

5

Dublin and Portarlington *see* under **Dublin** and **Leix** in the **COUNTIES** section below

Immigration: *Letters of denization ... England and Ireland 1603-1700*, by W.A. Shaw (Huguenot Society of London, vol. 18, 1911), and *1710-1800*, by W.A. Shaw (Huguenot Society of London, vol. 27, 1923) with Supplement (Huguenot Society of London, vol. 35, 1932) **[all HUG/PER]**. *The Scottish migration to Ulster in the reign of James I*, by M. Perceval-Maxwell (1973) **[IR/G 213]**. 'Scottish migration to Ireland during the early modern period 1603-1720' by M. Maxwell, in *Anglo-Celtic Annals: proceedings of the BIFHSGO Conference* (1996) **[CAN/ON/PER]**. *The rise and fall of Parkgate, passenger port for Ireland, 1686-1815*, ed. G.W. Place (Chetham Society, Third Series, vol. 39, 1994) **[LA/PER]**. *See also* **Huguenots** above and **Jews** and **Palatines** below

Interests: *Ulster genealogical & historical guild: subscribers' interest list (Directory of Irish family history research), No. 14* ed. B. Trainor & J. Passmore (Belfast, 1991) **[IR/PER]**. *An teolai: the Irish Family History Society research directory*, vol. 1 (Dun Laoghaire Genealogical Society, 1993) **[Apply to staff]**

Jews: *The Jews of Ireland from earliest times to ... 1910*, by L. Hyman (London & Jerusalem, 1972) **[JR/GEN]**. 'Jewish genealogy in Ireland', by A. Benson, in *Aspects of Irish genealogy* (1993) **[IR/G 194]**

Justices of the Peace *see* **Officials**

Landed Gentry *see* **Pedigrees**

Lawyers: *King's Inn admission papers 1607-1867* ed. E. Keane, P.B. Phair & T.U. Sadleir (Dublin, 1982) **[IR/G 59]**. *The [Irish] Incorporated Law Society's calendar and law directory 1915* **[PR/LAW]**. Commissioners of affidavits & notaries public in Ireland 1796, in *Some Irish lists*, vol. 1 **[IR/G 123]**. *See also* **Officials**

Magistrates *see* **Officials**

Maps: *A topographical dictionary of Ireland*, by S. Lewis (2 vols., London, 1846) **[TB/GAZ and IR/G 188-9]**. *Cassell's Gazetteer of Great Britain & Ireland*, vols. 1-6 (1893-8) **[TB/GAZ]**. *Genealogical atlas of Ireland*, by D.E. Gardner, D. Harland & F. Smith (Salt Lake City, 1964) **[IR/G 1]**. *Irish county maps showing the locations of churches in Leinster province* (Salt Lake City, 1977) [includes Carlow, Dublin, Dublin City, Kildare, Kilkenny, Leix (Queens), Longford, Louth, Meath, Offaly (Kings), Westmeath, Wexford, Wicklow] **[IR/L 60]**. *A new genealogical atlas of Ireland*, by B. Mitchell (Baltimore, 1986) **[IR/G 133]**. For maps of specific areas *see* the **Local History** entries in the **COUNTIES** section below. *See also* **Ordnance Survey Memoirs** below

Newspapers: *A handlist of Irish newspapers 1685-1750*, by R.L. Munter (London, 1960) **[IR/G 67]**. *Northern Ireland newspapers 1737-1987: a checklist with locations* (Belfast, 1987) **[IR/G 147]**. *Newspapers: their whereabouts and uses*, by M. Casteleyn (1994) **[Audio cassette]**

Nurses: *Register of nurses, 1937* (Dublin, 1937) **[IR/G 121]**

Officials: Coroners of Ireland 1796, in *Some Irish lists*, vol. 1 **[IR/G 123]**. Custodians of public records, Ireland, 1791-1823, in *Some Irish lists*, vol. 7 **[IR/G 129]**. High sheriffs of Ireland, 1742-1816, in *Some Irish lists*, vol. 2 **[IR/G 124]**. Justices of the Peace for Ireland 1797, in *Some Irish lists*, vol. 1 **[IR/G 123]**. Justices of the Peace for Ireland 1837, in *Some Irish lists*, vol. 1 **[IR/G 123]**. Magistrates of cities & corporate towns in Ireland, October 1736, in *Some Irish lists*, vol. 2 **[IR/G 124]**. *The Irish Parliament 1775*, ed. W. Hunt (Dublin, 1907) **[IR/G 14]**. *See also* **Patent Rolls**

Old Age Pension Claims: *Ireland: old age pension claims name index Part 1 and 2: 1841-51 census abstracts & miscellaneous sources, including an introduction to the claims & guide to the name index* [abstracts created 1908-22 from census returns; claimants and relatives born 1750s-1864, mainly in Ulster], by J.B. Brooks (Mfc, 1994-6) **[Shelf 9]**

Orders: *The Most Illustrious Order of St Patrick 1783-1983*, by P. Galloway (1983) **[IR/G 184]**. *Awards of the Medal of the Order of the British Empire for Gallantry in Ireland, 1920-2* by M.D. Cassell (1986) **[ARMY]**. *See also* **Templars**

Ordnance Survey Maps: for individual maps *see* the **Local History** entries in the **COUNTIES** section below

Ordnance Survey Memoirs of Ireland, ed. A. Day, P. McWilliams, &c. (40 vols., 1990-7) **[IR/G 103-42]**. For the individual volumes *see* the **Local History** entries for **Antrim, Armagh, Cavan, Donegal, Down, Fermanagh, Leitrim, Londonderry, Louth, Monaghan, Sligo** and **Tyrone** in the **COUNTIES** section below

Palatines: *The Palatine families of Ireland*, by H.Z. Jones (Camden, Maine, 1990) **[IR/G 136]**. *Irish Palatine Association Newsletter*, vol. 1, no. 1 (1990) to date **[IR/PER]**

Parliament *see* **Officials**

Patent Rolls: *Patentee officers in Ireland 1173-1826, including High Sheriffs 1661-1684 & 1761-1816* ed. J.L.J. Hughes (Dublin, 1960) **[IR/G 70]**. *Irish Patent Rolls of James I* (Irish Record Commission, 1830; reprinted 1966) **[IR/GEN Folio]**. *Irish Patent Rolls of James I: index of persons*, by P. Manning (TS, 1987) **[IR/G 142]**

Pedigrees: *The Irish and Anglo-Irish landed gentry when Cromwell came to Ireland*, by J. O'Hart (Dublin, 1884) **[IR/G 63]**. *Irish pedigrees of the origin and stem of the Irish nation*, by J. O'Hart (3rd ed., Dublin, 1881 **[IR/G 60]**; 5th ed. 2 vols., Dublin, 1892 **[IR/G 61-2]**). *Genealogical tracts 1: A. The introduction to the book of genealogies; B. The ancient tract on the distribution of the Aithech-thuatha; C. The Lecan miscellany*, ed. T. O Raithbheartaig (Irish Manuscripts Commission, 1932) **[IR/G 216]**. *Corpus genealogiarum Hiberniae*, ed. M.A. O'Brian (vol. 1, Dublin, 1962) **[IR/G 71]**. *Visitation of Ireland* ed. J.J. Howard & F.A. Crisp (6 vols., London, 1897-1918) **[FH/MISC]**. *Burke's genealogical and heraldic history of the landed gentry of Ireland* (1st edn. 1899; 2nd edn. 1904; 3rd edn. 1912; 4th edn., London, 1958) **[all P/R/LST]**. *Burke's Irish family records* (London, 1976) **[P/R/LST]**

Peerage, &c: *The peerage of Ireland*, by John Lodge (1750) revised by Mervyn Archdall (7 vols., Dublin, 1789) **[P/R]**. Many standard works on the Peerage/Royalty Shelves contain details of Irish Peers; all appear in *The complete peerage* (13 vols. 1910-59) **[P/R]**

Pension Claims *see* **Old Age Pension Claims**

Place Names: *The origin and history of Irish names of places*, by P.W. Joyce, vol. 1 (5th edn. 1883) **[IR/G 155]**, vols. 1-3 (facsimile reprint, 1995) **[IR/G 201-3]**. *The master book of Irish place names: place name locator and master atlas of Ireland*, by M. O'Laughlin (1994) **[IR/G 197]**. *Place names of Great Britain and Ireland*, by J. Field (Newton Abbot, 1970) **[TB/PN]**

Police: *Royal Irish Constabulary list and directory: containing a list of the constabulary departments, resident magistrates, Dublin metropolitan police, coast guards &c.* (22 vols., 1881, 1884-5, 1890-1902, 1904-8) **[PR/POL]**. *Royal Irish Constabulary index, Part 1, 1816-82*, by Hervey Bay Indexers (Mfc, 1993) **[Apply to staff]**. *Royal Irish Constabulary index, Part 2, 1882-*

1921, by V. Gumley, B. Close & J. Reakes (Mfc, 1992) **[Apply to staff]**. 'Policemen in your family tree' by Gregory Allen, in *Aspects of Irish genealogy* (1993) **[IR/G 194]**

Population: *The population of Ireland 1750-1845*, by K.H. Connell (1950, reprinted 1975) **[IR/G 191]**

Portraits: *Irish portraits 1660-1860*, by A. Crookshank and the Knight of Glin (1969) **[IR/G 120]**

Presbyterians: *History of the congregations in the Presbyterian church in Ireland 1610-1982* (Belfast, 1982) **[IR/G 167]** also its *Supplement of additions, emendations and corrections ... and an index* (Belfast, 1996) **[IR/G 167A]**. *Fasti of the General Assembly of the Presbyterian Church in Ireland 1840-1910*, by J.M. Barkley & A Loughridge (Belfast, 1986-7) **[IR/G 180]**, bound with *Fasti of the Reformed Presbyterian Church in Ireland Part 1*, by J.M. Barkley & A. Loughridge (Belfast, 1970) **[IR/G 180]**

Printers: *A dictionary of the print trade in Ireland 1550-1775*, by R. Munter (1988) **[IR/G 195]**

Prisoners: *List of all persons detained in prison under the Statute 44 Vict. c. 4 (Protection of Person and Property (Ireland) Act, 1881) ... [1 April 1882 & June 1882]* **[MF 2834]**

Public Records: *A short guide to the principal classes of documents preserved in the Public Record Office, Dublin*, by R.H. Murray (1919) **[Store A]**. *A guide to the public records deposited in the Public Record Office of Ireland*, by H. Wood (1919) **[Store A]**. *Reports of the Deputy Keeper of Public Records*, Dublin (vols. 17-57, 1885-1931) **[IR/K]** and Belfast (1924-1937) **[IR/K]**. *Report of the Deputy Keeper of the Records (of Northern Ireland)* 1966-72 **[IR/G 163]**, 1981-86 **[IR/G 164]** (Belfast, 1988-9). *Directory of Irish archives* ed. S. Helferty & R. Refausse (Dublin, 1988) **[Enquiry Desk, Shelf 8]**, (2nd edn. 1993) **[Quick reference shelves]**. *Irish history from 1700: a guide to sources in the Public Record Office [London]*, by A. Prochaska (London, 1986) **[Enquiry Desk, Shelf 8]**. *Beginners' National Archives [Dublin]*, by G. O'Connor (1994) **[Audio cassette]**. *National Archives [Dublin]*, by K. Hannigan **[Audio cassette]**. *Beginners' Public Record Office of Northern Ireland*, by R. Strong (1994) **[Audio cassette]**. *Public Record Office of Northern Ireland*, by I. Maxwell (1994) **[Audio cassette]**. *See also* **Officials** above

Quakers: *Quakers in Ireland 1654-1900*, by I. Grubb (1927) **[IR/G 77]**. *Guide to Irish Quaker records 1654-1860*, by O.C. Goodbody (Dublin, 1967) **[IR/G 75]**. *The annual monitor, or obituary of the members of the Society of Friends in Great Britain & Ireland*, New Series, Nos. 23-43 (1865-85), 45-52 (1887-94), 97 (1910), 101 (1913) and 105 (1917) **[all QU/PER]**. *See also* **Friends Meeting House** in the WILLS section below

Railways: *Irish railways since 1916*, by M.H.C. Baker (London, 1972) **[IR/G 145]**

Research: *A simple guide to Irish genealogy*, by W. Clare (1938) **[IR/G 190]**. *Sources of Irish local history*, by T.P. O'Neill (Dublin, 1958) **[Ireland Tracts 1]**. *Irish and Scotch-Irish ancestral research*, by M.D. Falley (2 vols., Evanston, 1961-2) **[IR/G 41-2]**. *A simple guide to Irish genealogy*, by R. ffolliott (London, 1966) **[IR/G 175]**. *Handbook on Irish genealogy: how to trace your ancestors and relatives in Ireland*, by D.F. Begley (6th ed., Dublin, 1984) **[Enquiry Desk, Shelf 8]**. *Burke's introduction to Irish ancestry* ed. H. Montgomery-Massingberd (London, 1976) **[IR/G 40]**. *Irish genealogy: a record finder*, by D.F. Begley (Dublin, 1981) **[Enquiry Desk, Shelf 8]**. *The ancestor trail in Ireland: a companion guide*, by D.F. Begley (Dublin, 1982)

[IR/G 39]. *A genealogical research guide for Ireland,* by the Genealogical Department of the Church of Jesus Christ of Latter-day Saints (Salt Lake City, 1984) [IR/G 192A]. *A guide to Irish roots,* by W. & M. Dunning (California, 1986) [IR/G 141]. *Tracing Irish catholic families,* by P. Gorry (1986) [Audio cassette]. *How to trace family history in Northern Ireland,* by K. Neill (Belfast, 1986) [IR/G 15]. *Irish records: sources for family & local history,* by J.G. Ryan (Salt Lake City, 1988) [Enquiry Desk, Shelf 8]. *Directory of Irish genealogy,* by S. Murphy (3 vols., Dublin, 1990 [Enquiry Desk, Shelf 8], 1991 [Enquiry Desk, Shelf 8], 1993 [IR/GEN]). *Sources in England for Irish genealogy,* by M. Casteleyn (1990) [Audio cassette]. *The Irish roots guide,* by T. McCarthy (Dublin, 1991) [IR/G 174]. *Aspects of Irish genealogy: proceedings of the 1st Irish Genealogical Congress,* ed. M.D. Evans & E. O Duill (1993) [IR/G 194]. *Tracing your Irish ancestors: the complete guide,* by J. Grenham (Dublin, 1992) [IR/G 178]. *Introduction to Irish research: Irish ancestry: a beginner's guide,* by B. Davis (FFHS, 1992) [IR/G 181]. 'Tracing family history in Ireland: guides and information sources' by J.H. Lynn, in *Anglo-Celtic Annals: proceedings of the BIFHSGO Conference* (1996) [CAN/ON/PER]. *Going to Ireland: a genealogical researcher's guide,* by S. Irvine & N.M. Hickey (1997) [Enquiry Desk, Shelf 9]. *Beginners' introduction to Irish genealogical research,* by C. O'Flaherty (1994) [Audio cassette]. *The Irish Genealogical Project,* by A. Brennan (1994) [Audio cassette]. *Beginners' National Library,* by E. O Duill (1994) [Audio cassette]. *Civil records: Dublin, Belfast & county repositories,* by J. Grenham (1994) [Audio cassette]. *Irish estate papers,* by J. McCabe (1994) [Audio cassette]. *Land Commission records,* by O. Warke (1994) [Audio cassette]. *Land records of the 19th century,* by T. McCarthy (1994) [Audio cassette]. *National Library of Ireland,* by W. Buckley (1994) [Audio cassette]. *Quit Rent Office,* by E. Ellie (1994) [Audio cassette]. *Records of the former State Paper Office,* by T. Quinlan (1994) [Audio cassette]. *State Papers of Ireland: 13th-17th centuries,* by J. Walton (1994) [Audio cassette]. *Registry of Deeds,* by T.P. O'Neill (1994) [Audio cassette]. *When the going gets tough: Ulster sources 1600-1850,* by T. Parkhill (1994) [Audio cassette]. There are also specialised guides to research in Donegal, Dublin, Kerry, Kilkenny and Meath; *see* under LOCAL in the COUNTIES section below

Royal Irish Constabulary *see* **Police**

Schools: *Home education: or Irish versus English grammar schools for Irish boys,* by M.C. Hime (London, 1887) [IR/G 29]. *National school system 1831-1924: facsimile documents,* by K. Hannigan (Dublin, 1984) [IR/G 179]. For individual school registers and histories *see* under SCHOOLS in the COUNTIES section below

Societies *see* **Associations**

Surgeons: *History of the Royal College of Surgeons in Ireland and of the Irish schools of medicine including numerous biographical sketches,* by C.A. Cameron (1886) [IR/G 165]

Surnames: *Special report on surnames in Ireland,* by R.E. Matheson (Dublin, 1894) [IR/G 78]. *Some anglicised surnames in Ireland,* by P.M. Giolla-Domhnaigh (Dublin, 1923) [Ireland Tracts 1]. *Some Ulster surnames,* by P.M. Domhnaigh (1923, revised Dublin, 1974) [Ireland Tracts 1]. *Irish names and surnames,* by P. Woulfe (reprinted 1967) [Shelf 3; duplicate IR/G 186]. *Irish families, their names, arms and origins,* by E. MacLysaght (Dublin, 1957) [IR/G 35]. *More Irish families: a new revised and enlarged edition of*

More Irish families, incorporating Supplement to Irish families, with an essay on Irish chieftainries, by E. MacLysaght (Dublin, 1982) **[IR/G 36]**. *Irish family names; highlights of 50 family histories*, by I. Grehan (London, 1973) **[IR/G 38]**. *Ten thousand saints: a study in Irish & European origins*, by H. Butler (Kilkenny, 1972) **[IR/G 43]**. *The surnames of Ireland*, by E. MacLysaght (Dublin, 1985) **[IR/G 79]**. *The book of Ulster surnames*, by R. Bell (Belfast, 1988) **[IR/G 160]**. *Clans and families of Ireland and Scotland: an ethnography of the Gael, A.D.500-1750*, by C.T. Cairney (Jefferson, N.C., 1989) **[IR/G 154]**. *The surnames of Derry*, by B. Mitchell (1992) **[IR/L 171]**. *The master book of Irish surnames: locations, ethnic origins, variant spellings and sources*, by M. O'Laughlin (1993) **[IR/G 166]**. *English surnames in Ireland*, by G. Redmonds (1994) **[Audio cassette]**

Surveys: *A concluding memoir on manuscript, mapped and other townland surveys in Ireland, 1688-1864*, by Mr. Hardinge (n.p., n.d.) **[IR/G 176]**. *See also* **Civil Survey** and **Griffiths Valuation** above

Templars: 'Documents relating to the suppression of the Templars in Ireland', by G. MacNiocaill, in *Analecta Hibernica*, no. 24 (Irish Manuscripts Commission, 1967) **[IR/PER]**

Universities. *See* **Dublin**, **Belfast** and **Galway** in the **COUNTIES** section below; *see also* **Schools** above

Workhouses: *The workhouses of Ireland: the fate of Ireland's poor*, by J. O'Connor (1995) **[IR/G 200]**. *See also* **Hospitals** above

---

PARISH AND NONCONFORMIST REGISTERS

General Guides: *A guide to Irish parish registers*, by B. Mitchell (Baltimore, 1988) **[Enquiry Desk, Shelf 8]**. *List of 110 Church of Ireland parishes in the province of Ulster with pre-1800 vestry minute books noting dates of commencement, the earliest date of baptismal registers ...* (n.d.) **[Box 86, Folder 29]**. *Draft sectional list of parish registers in Northern Ireland compiled for the Northern Ireland Record Office* (TS, 1968) **[IR/R 6]**. *A guide to Irish churches and graveyards*, by B. Mitchell (Baltimore, 1990) **[Enquiry Desk, Shelf 8; IR/G 157]**. *Handlist of Church of Ireland parish registers in the Representative Church Body Library, Dublin*, by R. Refausse (TS, 1991) **[IR/R 10]**. *Directory of parish registers indexed in Ireland: Irish FHS Issue No. 1* (1992) **[Enquiry Desk, Shelf 8]**; *Issue No. 2* (1994) **[Enquiry Desk, Shelf 8]**; *Issue No. 3* (1997) **[Enquiry Desk, Shelf 9]**. *Irish church records: their history, availability and use in family and local history research*, ed. J.G. Ryan (1992) **[IR/R 151]**. *An Irish genealogical source: guide to church records* [a list of all church records held in PRONI for the former Province of Ulster], by Public Record Office of Northern Ireland (1994) **[IR/R 35]**. *Protestant church records in Ireland*, by B. Trainor (1986) **[Audio cassette]**. Copies of individual registers are listed in the **COUNTIES** section below. These are Church of Ireland registers unless otherwise stated

Composite Indexes: International Genealogical Index of Births, Baptisms and Marriages, compiled by the Genealogical Society of Utah (207 Microfiche, 1992; includes all births in Ireland 1864-67) **[Lower Library]**. *Irish marriages, being an index to the marriages in Walker's Hibernian Magazine, 1771-1812*, by H. Farrar (2 vols., London, 1897) **[IR/R 1-2]**. *Index to births, marriages & deaths in ... the Hibernian Chronicle, Oct 1769-1802 [sic]* (TS), vol. 1, 1769-

72 [IR/R 32], vol. 2, 1773-5 [IR/R 33]. *Index to persons mentioned in the Hibernian Chronicle 1776-1780* (MS, 1947) [IR/G 224]

MARRIAGE LICENCES

PREROGATIVE COURT OF ARMAGH
Betham's Abstracts of Prerogative Court of Armagh Marriage Licences 1629-1810 [MF 324-325]

CONSISTORY COURTS
Clonfert: *Index to Clonfert Marriage Licence Bonds, Wills and Administration Bonds* supplement to *Irish ancestor* (1970) [IR/R 4]
Cloyne: *Index to the Marriage Licence Bonds of the Diocese of Cloyne 1630-1800*, by T.G.H. Green (1899-1900) [IR/R 3]
Cork and Ross: *Index to the Marriage Licence Bonds of the Diocese of Cork and Ross 1623-1750*, by H.W. Gillman (1896-7) [IR/R 3]. *12,128 Marriage License Bonds, Diocese of Cork and Ross, County of Cork, Ireland*, by A.E. Casey (TS, 1963) [IR/G 196]
Dublin: Dublin Marriage Licences 1536-1800 and 1800-1858, Appendixes to 26th (1895) and 30th (1899) Reports of Deputy Keeper [IR/G 72 and duplicate at IR/G 219; IR/K]. Betham's Abstracts of Dublin Marriage Licences 1638-1824 [MF 326-331]
Killaloe: 'Killaloe Marriage Licence Bonds 1680-1720 and 1760-1762' in *Irish genealogist*, vol. 5 (1974-9) 580-90 [IR/PER]. 'A list of entries of Marriage Licence Grants in Killaloe Court and Register Book 1776-1845' in *Irish genealogist*, vol. 5 (1974-9) 710-9 [IR/PER]
Limerick: *Marriage Bonds for Diocese of Limerick* Index for 1844 only (TS) [IR/R 25]
Ossory: 'Ossory Marriage Licence Bonds (Extracts) 1669-1823' in *Irish genealogist* vol. 4, no. 4 (1971) [IR/PER]
Raphoe: *Index to Raphoe Marriage Licence Bonds 1710-55 & 1817-30*, by R. ffolliott, supplement to *Irish ancestor* (1969) [IR/R 5]
Miscellaneous: 'Marriage Licence Bonds ... in the Jennings MSS in Dublin', by J.C. Walton in *Decies*, no. 24 (Sep. 1983) [Box 86, Folder 34]

MONUMENTAL INSCRIPTIONS

General: *A guide to Irish churches and graveyards*, by B. Mitchell (Baltimore, 1990) [IR/G 157] attempts to list all known graveyards. *Journal of the Association for the Preservation of the Memorials of the Dead in Ireland* vols. 2-10 (Dublin, 1892-1920) [IR/M 2-11], continued as *Journal of the Irish Memorials Association*, vols. 11, 12 (Parts 5-6) and 13 (Parts 1-2) (Dublin, 1921-37) [IR/PER] has many inscriptions from churches and churchyards throughout Ireland. *An index of the churchyards and buildings ... in the Journal of the Association for the Preservation of the Memorials of the Dead in Ireland 1888-1908* (Dublin, 1909) [IR/M 11] lists the places covered up to 1908. See also *Irish church monuments 1570-1880*, by H. Potterton (1975) [IR/M 30]. *Some funeral entries in Ireland c.1632-1729*, ed. W. FitzGerald [IR/M 23]. 'Funeral certificates of Ireland' by J. Foster, in *Collectanea genealogica*, vol. 7 (1882) [PER/COL].

11

Copies: copies of the inscriptions in individual churches, churchyards and cemeteries are listed in the **COUNTIES** section below. These copies are not necessarily complete. Full bibliographical details of those acquired before 1987 are given in *Monumental inscriptions in the library of the Society of Genealogists: Part II: Northern England, Wales, Scotland, Ireland, and Overseas*, by L. Collins and M. Morton (London, 1987).

LISTS AND DIRECTORIES WITH NATIONAL COVERAGE

1738, 1739, 1740, 1741, 1742, 1743, 1747, 1748, 1749, 1750, 1752, 1753, 1754, 1755, 1756, 1757, 1758, 1760, 1761, 1762, 1764, 1765, 1767, 1768, 1769, 1770, 1771 (27 vols.) *Watson's Gentleman's and citizen's almanack*, in *The gentleman's almanack* **[ALM]**

1771 Wives certificate book, Benevolent Annuity Company, 21 Mch 1771, in *Some Irish lists*, vol. 7 **[IR/G 129]**

1772, 1773, 1774, 1775, 1776, 1777 **[Apply to staff]**, 1778, 1779, 1780, 1781 **[Apply to staff]**, 1782, 1783 **[Apply to staff]**, 1784, 1785, 1786, 1787, 1788, 1789 **[Apply to staff]**, 1790 (19 vols.) *Watson's Gentleman's and citizen's almanack*, in *The gentleman's almanack* **[ALM]**

1790   A list of pensions on the Irish establishment 1790, in *Some Irish lists*, vol. 5 **[IR/G 127]**

1792   *Watson's Gentleman's and citizen's almanack*, in *The gentleman's almanack* **[ALM]**

1793   *Watson's Gentleman's and citizen's almanack*, in *The treble almanack* **[ALM]**

1796   *Surname index for the 1796 spinning wheel premium entitlement lists of Ireland* (Mfc, 1986) **[Apply to staff]**

1795, 1796, 1797, 1798, 1799, 1800, 1801, 1802, 1803, 1804, 1805, 1806, 1807, 1808, 1809, 1810, 1811, 1812, 1814, 1815 **[also on Mfc, apply to staff]**, 1816, 1817, 1818, 1819, 1820 (25 vols.) *Watson Stewart's Gentleman's and citizen's almanack*, in *The treble almanack* **[ALM]**

1820   *The general directory of Newry, Armagh & the towns of Dungannon, Portadown, Tandragee, Lurgan, Waringstown, Banbridge, Warrenpoint, Rosstrevor, Kilteel, Ruthfriland etc.*, by Thomas Bradshaw (1819, reprinted 1984) **[IR/D 1820]**

1821, 1822, 1823 (3 vols.) *Watson Stewart's Gentleman's and citizen's almanack*, in *The treble almanack* **[ALM]**

1824   *Pigot & Co's City of Dublin and Hibernian provincial directory* (London, 1824) **[Enquiry Desk, Shelf 7]**

1824, 1825 (2 vols.) *Watson Stewart's Gentleman's and citizen's almanack*, in *The treble almanack* **[ALM]**

1826, 1827, 1828, 1829 **[also on Mfc, apply to staff]**, 1830, 1831, 1832, 1833, 1834 (9 vols.) *Watsons' or The gentleman's & citizen's almanack*, in *The treble almanack* **[ALM]**

1835   *Pettigrew & Oulton's Dublin almanac & general register of Ireland* **[ALM]**

1835, 1837, 1838 (3 vols.) *Watsons' or The gentleman's & citizen's almanack*, in *The treble almanack* **[ALM]**

1840, 1845, 1846 (3 vols.) *Pettigrew & Oulton's Dublin almanac & general register of Ireland* **[ALM]**

1844-60 Griffith's Valuation; *see* above in **GENERAL** section

1846   *Slater's national commercial directory of Ireland* (Manchester, 1846) **[Enquiry Desk, Shelf 7; *also* Mfc]**

1849   *Thom's Irish almanac & official directory, with the Post Office Dublin city and county directory* **[Apply to staff]**

1852	*Thom's Irish almanac & official directory of the United Kingdon of Great Britain & Ireland with the Post Office Dublin city and county directory* **[IR/D 1852]**
1868	*Thom's Irish almanac & official directory of the United Kingdom of Great Britain & Ireland with the Post Office Dublin city and County directory* **[Mfc, apply to staff]**
1871	*Thom's Irish almanac & official directory of the United Kingdom of Great Britain & Ireland* **[IR/D 1871]**
1876	*Return of owners of land of one acre and upwards, in the several counties of cities, and counties of towns in Ireland* (Dublin, 1876) **[IR/G 65]**
1877	*Thom's Irish almanac & official directory of the United Kingdom of Great Britain & Ireland with the Post Office Dublin city and County directory* **[Mfc, apply to staff]**
1881	*Slater's royal national commercial directory of Ireland including, in addition to the trades list, alphabetical directories of Dublin, Belfast, Cork & Limerick* **[Mfc, apply to staff]**
1905	*Kelly's Directory of Ireland* (London, 1905) **[IR/D 11-12]**
1908	*Porter's Guide to the manufacturers and shippers of Ireland* by F. Porter (Belfast, 1908) **[IR/D 13]**
1908	*Thom's Official directory of the United Kingdom of Great Britain & Ireland ... & Post Office Dublin city & county directory* **[IR/D 1908]**
1909	*Thom's Official directory of the United Kingdom of Great Britain & Ireland ... & Post Office Dublin city & county directory* **[Apply to staff]**
1925	*The Irish motorists' directory* by J.J. Blake (Dublin, 1925) **[IR/D 10]**
1953	*Thom's Directory of Ireland for the year 1953, comprising Republic of Ireland ..., Northern Ireland ...* (Dublin, 1953) **[IR/D 6]**
1963	*Eolai telefoin na hEirann: the Irish telephone directory, October 1963* (Dublin, 1963) **[IR/D 8]**
1973-4	*Kelly's Manufacturing & merchant directory, vol. 1, United Kingdom and Republic of Ireland* **[Apply to staff]**
1983	*Eolai telefoin na hEirann: the Ireland telephone directory, 1983* (2 vols., Dublin, 1983) **[IR/D 8]**
1983	*Northern Ireland (Section 241) telephone directory, May 1983* (Mfc., London, 1983) **[Apply to staff]**
1985	*Ireland: a directory* (Dublin, Institute of Public Administration, 1985) **[IR/D 19]**
1989	*Northern Ireland phone book, Section 241, May 1989* (Mfc., London, 1983) **[Apply to staff]**
1990-1	*Eolai telefon na hEireann: the Ireland telephone directory* **[Apply to staff]**

PERIODICALS

Analecta Hibernica, vols. 2 (1931), 3, 7, 17, 20, 22, 24, 25 only **[IR/PER]**

History Ireland, vol. 2, no. 3 (1994) to date **[IR/PER]**

The Irish ancestor, vol. 1 (1969) to vol. 18 (1986) **[IR/PER]**

Irish ancestors matters, vol. 1, nos. 1 & 2 (Dublin, 1992-3) **[Ireland Tracts 1]**

The Irish at home and abroad: a journal of Irish genealogy and heritage, vol. 2, no. 1 (1994) to date **[IR/PER]**

The Irish genealogist: official organ of the Irish Genealogical Research Society, vol. 1 (London, 1937) to date **[IR/PER]**

Irish Palatine Association Newsletter, vol. 1, no. 1 (1990) to date **[IR/PER]**

Irish roots, nos. 1 & 2 (1992) **[IR/PER]**

The Irish sword, vols. 1-3 (1949-1957) **[IR/PER]**

Journal of Royal Society of Antiquaries of Ireland, vols. 21-61 (1890-1931) not complete **[IR/PER]**

North Irish roots, vol. 1 (1984) to date **[IR/PER]**.

WILLS

PREROGATIVE COURT OF ARMAGH
Surviving Originals: list of surviving Original Wills & Copies, *55th Report of Deputy Keeper* (1928) 30 **[IR/K]**; index of surviving Will Books, *56th Report of Deputy Keeper* (1931) 79-197 **[IR/K]**; index of 2nd and 3rd surviving Grant Books, *57th Report of Deputy Keeper* (1935) 62-324 **[IR/K]**

Abstracts: Microfilms of Sir William Betham's abstracts of wills 1530-1808 **[MF 309-16]**, administrations 1595-1810 **[MF 317-23]** and letters of tutelage 1595-1754 **[MF 324]** from PRO Dublin. Pedigrees from abstracts **[MF 333]**

Index: *Index to the Prerogative Wills of Ireland 1538-1810*, ed. Sir Arthur Vicars (Dublin, 1897) **[IR/G 93; another copy IR/G 150]**

CONSISTORY COURTS
Ardagh: will index 1695-1858, supplement to *Irish ancestor* (Dublin, 1971) **[IR/G 81]**

Ardfert and Aghadoe: will index 1690-1800 (*Phillimore indexes to Irish wills*, vol.3, London, 1913) **[IR/G 84]**

Cashel and Emly: will indexes 1618-1800 (*Phillimore indexes to Irish wills*, vol. 3, London, 1913) **[IR/G 84]**

Clonfert: will index 1663-1857 (with index of administration bonds 1738-1857 and Marriage Licence Bonds), supplement to *Irish ancestor* (1970) **[Ireland Tracts 1]**; variant version 1663-1838, by I.A.P. Smythe-Wood (n.p., 1977) **[IR/G 139]**

Cloyne: will index 1621-1800 (*Phillimore indexes to Irish wills*, vol. 2, London, 1910) **[IR/G 84]**. *Index to 2,709 administration bonds, Diocese of Cloyne, County of Cork, Ireland, 1630-1857*, by A.E. Casey (TS, 1963) **[IR/G 196]**

Connor: index to will and grant books, 1818-1858, *56th Report of Deputy Keeper* (1931) 79-197 **[IR/K]**

Cork & Ross: will index 1548-1800 (*Phillimore indexes to Irish wills*, vol. 2, London, 1910) **[IR/G 84]**; further version 1611-1803 & 1818-1833 in *Cork archaeological journal*, 2nd Series, vols. 1-4 (1895-8) **[IR/PER]**. Wills listed 1547-1628 in *Cork archaeological journal*, 2nd series, vol. 1 (1895) 186-7 **[IR/PER]**, are abstracted in *The gentleman's magazine* 1861 (i, 530; ii, 33, 257, 501) and 1862 (i, 28, 165, 439, 710; ii, 299) **[PER/GEN]**. *Index to 3,735 Prerogative Wills, Ireland 1536-1810 relating to Cork and Kerry [D-Z only]*, by A.E. Casey (TS, 1963) **[IR/G 196]**. *Index to 8,250 administration bonds, Diocese of Cork, County of Cork, 1612-1858*, by A.E. Casey (TS, 1963) **[IR/G 196]**

Derry: will index 1615-1858 (*Phillimore indexes to Irish wills*, vol. 5, London, 1920) **[IR/G 84]**

Down: index to will and grant books 1850-1858, *56th Report of Deputy Keeper* (1931) 79-197 **[IR/K]**

Dromore: will index 1678-1858 (*Phillimore indexes to Irish wills*, vol. 4, London, 1918) **[IR/G 84]**

Dublin: abstracts of wills and inventories 1457-1483, by H.F. Berry in *Royal Society of Antiquaries of Ireland, Extra Volume* (Dublin, 1898) **[IR/PER]**. Will index 1536-1800 and 1800-1858, Appendixes to 26th (1895) **[IR/G 72; duplicate at IR/G 219]** and 30th (1899) **[IR/K]** Reports of Deputy Keeper

Ferns: will index 1601-1800 (*Phillimore indexes to Irish wills*, vol. 1, London, 1909) **[IR/G 84]**

Kerry: *Index to 3735 Prerogative Wills, Ireland 1536-1810 relating to Cork and Kerry [D-Z only]*, by A.E. Casey (TS, 1963) **[IR/G 196]**

Kildare: will index 1661-1800 (*Phillimore indexes to Irish wills*, vol. 1, London, 1909) **[IR/G 84]** and 1678-1857 in *Journal of County Kildare Archaeological Society* vol. 4 (1905), no. 6 **[IR/PER]**. Index of administration bonds 1770-1848 in *Journal of*

County Kildare Archaeological Society, vol. 5 (1907), no. 3 **[IR/PER]**. Microfilm of abstracts of wills, by Sir William Betham A-K 1661-1826 (indexed) and K-S 1661-1824 (not indexed) **[MF 332]**

Killala and Achonry: will index 1698-1858, in *Irish genealogist*, vol. 3, no. 12 (1967) 506-19 **[IR/PER]**

Killaloe and Kilfenora: index of administration 1845 and caveats 1710-1723 in *57th Report of Deputy Keeper* (1935) 62-324 **[IR/K]**. Will index 1653-1800 (*Phillimore indexes to Irish wills*, vol. 3, London, 1913) **[IR/G 84]**

Kilmore: will index 1682-1857, by P. Smythe-Wood (n.p., 1975) **[IR/G 138]**

Leighlin: will index 1652-1800 (*Phillimore indexes to Irish wills*, vol. 1, London, 1909) **[IR/G 84]**. Index of administrations 1694-1845 in Supplement to *Irish ancestor* (1972) **[IR/G 134]**

Limerick: will index 1615-1800 (*Phillimore indexes to Irish wills*, vol. 3, London, 1913) **[IR/G 84]**

Newry and Mourne (Peculiar): will index 1727-1858 (*Phillimore indexes to Irish wills*, vol. 4, London, 1918) **[IR/G 84]**. Index of administrations 1811-1857 in *Irish ancestor*, vol. 1, no. 1 (1969) 41-2 **[IR/PER]**

Ossory: index to grant books 1848-1858, *57th Report of Deputy Keeper* (1935) 62-324 **[IR/K]**. Will Index 1536-1800 (*Phillimore indexes to Irish wills*, vol. 1, London, 1909) **[IR/G 84]**

Raphoe: will index 1684-1858 (*Phillimore indexes to Irish wills*, vol. 5, London, 1920) **[IR/G 84]**

Waterford and Lismore: will index 1645-1800 (*Phillimore indexes to Irish wills*, vol. 3, London, 1913) **[IR/G 84]**

OTHER TESTAMENTARY MATERIAL

Welply Collection: 18 volumes of *Irish wills and pleadings 1569-1859* **[IR/G 96-113]** & 1 volume *Pedigrees and Plea Rolls* **[IR/G 114]** abstracted by W.H. Welply (TS, 1921-33) with an every-name index (TS, 1985) **[IR/G 116]**. *Irish wills*, vol. 20 **[IR/G 115]**. Index to vol. 20 **[IR/G 117]**

Rosbottom Collection: abstracts of 4,000 Irish wills, by L. Rosbottom (TS & MS, 1986; *also* Mfc) **[apply to staff]**

Registry of Deeds: *Registry of Deeds, Dublin, Abstracts of Wills*, by P.B. Eustace, vol. 1 1708-1745 (Dublin, 1954) **[IR/G 90]**, vol. 2 1746-1785 (Dublin, 1955) **[IR/G 91]**, vol. 3 1785-1832 (Dublin, 1984) **[IR/G 131]**

Friends' Meeting House: *Quaker records, Dublin, abstracts of wills [1628-1795]*, by P.B. Eustace & O.C. Goodbody (Dublin, 1957) **[IR/G 76]**. Other Quaker wills 1664-1860 are abstracted in *Guide to Irish Quaker Records*, by O.C. Goodbody (Dublin, 1967) **[IR/G 75]**

Prerogative Court of Canterbury: *Abstracts of Irish wills before 1660 (with index to 1700) and Administrations 1559-1661*, by R.E.F. Garrett (TS, 1969) **[IR/G 94]**

National Archives, Dublin: 2,690 probate records received 1922-30, indexed in appendixes to *55th-57th Reports of Deputy Keeper* **[IR/K]**

Genealogical Office, formerly at Dublin Castle: index of 7,500 wills in various collections, compiled by P.B. Eustace, in *Analecta Hibernica*, no. 17 (Dublin, 1949) 147-348 **[IR/PER]**

Carrigan Manuscripts: index of 952 wills, mainly of Catholics in Diocese of Ossory 1546-1863, in *Irish genealogist*, vol. 4, no. 3 (1970) **[IR/PER]**

Swanzy Manuscripts: index of H.B. Swanzy collection of wills and administrations from Prerogative Court and Consistories of Clogher and Kilmore, 1681-1846, by P. Manning (TS, 1988) **[IR/G 143]**

Various Collections: *Irish genealogical guides: a calendar of wills in various collections that* *have escaped destruction*, by W. Clare (Dublin, 1930) **[IR/G 92]**. *Guide to copies and abstracts of Irish wills,* by W.G. Clare (1930) **[IR/G 118]**. For printed indexes to other collections see *Wills and their whereabouts*, by A.J. Camp (London, 1974) 222-4 **[TB/RG]** and *Will indexes and other probate material in the library of the Society of Genealogists*, by N. Newington-Irving (London, 1996) 51-7 **[WILLS/G; another copy TB/BIB]**

COUNTIES

ANTRIM

LISTS AND DIRECTORIES

c.1740 Adams's Directory of Belfast, in *North Irish roots*, vol. 4, no. 2 **[IR/PER]**

1744 City of Belfast Poll Book, in *The town book of the corporation of Belfast* (1892) **[IR/L 12]**

c.1800 Bigger's Merchants in the High Street of Belfast at the beginning of the 19th century, in *North Irish roots*, vol. 2, nos. 5 & 7 **[IR/PER]**

1805-07 *Holden's Triennial directory* (4th edn.), vol. 2, includes Belfast **[MF 2687 or MX/D 13]**

1805-08 *Holden's triennial directory* (4th edn. including the year 1808), vol. 2, includes Belfast **[MX/D 19]**

1807-8 *Merchants in plenty: Joseph Smyth's Belfast directories of 1807 & 1808 with an historical introduction & bibliography of Belfast directories to 1900* by J.R.R. Adams (1992) **[IR/D 1807-8]**

1832 *Smyth's Belfast almanac* **[IR/D 1832]**

1841-2 *Martin's Belfast directory for 1841-2* (reprint, 1992) **[IR/D 1842]**

1845 *Smyth's Belfast almanac* **[IR/D 1845]**

1861-2 *The Belfast and Province of Ulster directory for 1861-62*, vol. 5 **[IR/D 1861]**

1872 Millar's Old Ballymoney, in *North Irish roots*, vol. 2, no. 3 **[IR/PER]**

1873 *Street's Indian and colonial mercantile directory*, includes Belfast **[IND/D 13]**

1888 *County Antrim one hundred years ago: a guide and directory 1888* by G.H. Bassett (Belfast, 1989) **[IR/D 15]**

1892 *North Antrim: list of persons objected to ... 1892: polling district of Portrush* **[Box 86, Folder 41]**

1958 *Belfast News-Letter Directory of Belfast and Northern Ireland* (Belfast, 1958) **[IR/D 7]**

1989 *Belfast and Northern Ireland Directory* **[Apply to staff]**

LOCAL HISTORY

Maps: Ordnance Survey Maps: *Belfast (Central) 1931* (reprinted 1987) **[M 224]**; *Belfast: The Falls 1931* (reprinted 1989) **[M 309]**; *Belfast (North) 1920* (reprinted 1987) **[M 170]**; *Belfast (South) 1920* (reprinted 1989) **[M 434]**; *Lisburn 1902* (reprinted 1996) **[M 901]**

County: *Ordnance Survey Memoirs of Ireland*, ed. A. Day, P. McWilliams &c., vol. 2, *Parishes of County Antrim I 1838-9: Ballymartin, Ballyrobert, Ballywalter, Carnmoney, Mallusk* (Belfast & Dublin, 1990) **[IR/L 104]**; vol. 8, Antrim II 1832-8: Lisburn & South Antrim (1991) **[IR/L 110]**; vol. 10, Antrim III 1833, 1835, 1839-40: Larne & Island Magee (1991) **[IR/L 112]**; vol. 13, Antrim IV 1830-8: Glens of Antrim (1992) **[IR/L 115]**; vol. 16, Antrim V 1830-5, 1837-8: Giant's Causeway & Ballymoney (1992) **[IR/L 118]**; vol. 19, Antrim VI 1830, 1833, 1835-8: South-West Antrim (1993) **[IR/L 121]**; vol. 21, Antrim VII 1832-8: South Antrim (1993) **[IR/L 123]**. vol. 23, Antrim VIII 1831-5, 1837-8: Ballymena and West Antrim (1993) **[IR/L 125]**; vol. 24, Antrim IX 1830-2, 1835, 1838-9: North Antrim Coast and Rathlin (1994) **[IR/L 126]**. vol. 26, Antrim X 1830-1, 1833-5, 1839-40: East Antrim - Glynn, Inver, Kilroot, Templecorran (1995) **[IR/L 128]**; vol. 29, Antrim XI 1832-3, 1835-9: Antrim town and Ballyclare (Belfast, 1995) **[IR/L 131]**; vol. 32, Antrim XII 1832-3, 1835-40: Ballynure and district (1995) **[IR/L 134]**; vol. 35, Antrim XIII 1833, 1835, 1838: Templepatrick and district (1996) **[IR/L 137]**; vol. 37, Antrim XIV 1832, 1839-40: Carrickfergus (1996) **[IR/L 139]**. *Heads and hearths: the hearth money rolls and poll tax returns* *for co. Antrim 1660-69*, ed. S.T. Carleton (1991) **[IR/L 167]**

Ballyrashane: *Families of Ballyrashane: a district in Northern Ireland*, by T.H. Mullin (Belfast, 1969) **[IR/L 87]**

Belfast: Roll of burgesses 1613-1761, in Cary's *Some Irish lists*, vol. 6 **[IR/G 128]**. *The town book of the corporation of Belfast 1613-1816*, by R.M. Young (Belfast, 1892) [includes roll of burgesses 1635-1796] **[IR/L 12]** with MS index [missing 1987]. *Belfast and its charitable society: a story of urban social development*, by R.W.M. Strain (Oxford, 1961) **[IR/L 11]**. *Ulster Architectural Heritage Society list of historic buildings etc. [No. 1] vicinity of the Queens University of Belfast* (n.p., 1968) **[IR/PER]**. *Surname index to the 1860 Griffith's Valuation of the Municipal Borough of Belfast, Ireland*, by D.R. Hotaling (Mfc, 1988) **[apply to staff]**. *Griffith's Valuation of Smithfield & St Ann's Wards, Shankill, Belfast, 1860* **[IR/L 150]**

Carrickfergus: *Carrickfergus and its contacts: some chapters in the history of Ulster*, by J.F. MacNeice (London & Belfast, 1928) **[IR/L 84]**. 'Some executions in the county of Antrim' copied by H.N. Peyton (TS, 1954) from *The history and antiquities of the town of Carrickfergus*, by S. M'Skimm (1823) **[Box 86, Folder 21]**

Derrykeighan: *History of Derrykeighan parish for three centuries*, by T. Camac (n.p., 1930) **[IR/L 31]**

Lisburn: *Lisburn cathedral and its past rectors*, by W.P. Carmody (Belfast, 1926) **[IR/L 64]**

Rathlin Island: *Rathlin Island, north of Antrim*, by H.A. Boyd (Ballycastle, 1947) **[IR/L 74]**

MONUMENTAL INSCRIPTIONS

Ballycarry: non-subscribing Presbyterian graveyard **[IR/M 13]**.

Ballyclare: Presbyterian **[MF 697]**.

Ballygowan: RC graveyard **[IR/M 13]**; Knox Grave **[IR/M 13A]**

Ballykeel: graveyard **[IR/M 12]**

Ballynure: Old Graveyard **[IR/M 13A]**; Church of Ireland church **[IR/M 13A]**

Ballypriormore: graveyard **[IR/M 12]**

Ballyvallagh: gravestone **[IR/M 13]**

Belfast: Balmoral Cemetery, Friends' burial ground & Malone Presbyterian church and graveyard **[IR/M 24]**; Charitable Institution burial ground **[MF 694]**; Friar's Bush & Milltown graveyards **[IR/M 15]**; New Burying Ground, Clifton Street **[IR/M 29]**; Shankill graveyard & tablets in Christ Church & St George's Church **[IR/M 14]**

Bun-Na-Margy: Abbey churchyard (MS, 1911) **[Box 86, Folder 4]**

Carnmoney: Church of Ireland graveyard **[IR/M 33]**

Carrickfergus: Old Graveyard (St Nicholas'), St Nicholas' Church of Ireland church, Congregational church, First Presbyterian church, North Road Cemetery, St Nicholas' RC graveyard, Prospect RC Cemetery, Victoria Cemetery **[IR/M 13A]**

Culfeightrin: churchyard, in *Irish ancestor*, vol. 2, no. 2 (1970) 131-6 **[IR/PER]**

Derriaghy: Christ Church, church & churchyard **[Box 86, Folder 27]**

Glynn: graveyard **[IR/M 13]**

Islandmagee: graveyard **[IR/M 12]**

Killead: St Catherine churchyard **[Box 86, Folder 35]**

Kilroot: graveyard **[IR/M 13]**

Lambeg: churchyard (Belfast, 1937) **[Ireland Tracts 1]**

Loughmourne: Presbyterian graveyard **[IR/M 13A]**

Magheragall: churchyard, in *Family links*, vol. 1, no. 2 (1981) 31-32, and no. 3 (1981) 26-32 **[IR/PER]**

Raloo: graveyard, Church of Ireland graveyard, non-subscribing Presbyterian graveyard, Presbyterian graveyard **[IR/M 13]**

Straid: Congregational church **[IR/M 13A]**

Templecorran: graveyard, Church of Ireland graveyard **[IR/M 13]**

NEWSPAPERS
Belfast Magazine: obituary notices 1808-1811, in *Some Irish lists*, vol. 6 **[IR/G 128]**; marriages 1808-1814, in *Some Irish lists*, vol. 7 **[IR/G 129]**

Belfast News-Letter, July to December 1880 **[MF 2525-6]**

Belfast Protestant Journal, 4 May 1844 to 27 July 1850 **[MF 2527 & 2529]**

Belfast Telegraphic Circular: a mercantile & general newspaper, 13 March 1854 to 25 August 1855 **[MF 2530]**

Belfast Weekly Mail, 19 November 1852 to 15 September 1854 **[MF 2531]**

Weekly Press, Belfast, 29 January 1859 to 29 December 1860 **[MF 2567]**

PARISH REGISTERS
'List of co. Antrim registers by civil parish with their dates, denominations and (where known) their locations' in *Irish family links*, vol. 2, no. 8 (September 1986) **[Duplicate in Box 86, Folder 28]**.

Aghalee: 1811-45 extracts **[IR/R 31]**

Belfast: St Anne's Shankill (now Cathedral) M 1745-99 index, in *Irish Memorials Association*, vol. 13 **[IR/PER]**, CM 1825-44 extracts **[IR/R 28]**; Holy Trinity C 1844-77 **[IR/R 28]**; St George C 1817-70, M 1817-33 **[IR/R 27]**; St John *see* Malone; First Presbyterian Church C 1757-90, B 1712-36, lists 1642 & 1887 **[IR/R 29]**.

Blaris: 1714-23 extracts **[IR/R 31]**

Bushmills: Presbyterian C 1836-46, M 1824-26 extracts **[IR/R 31]**

Carrickfergus: some D 1853-1872 **[IR/M 13A]**

Derriaghy: C 1696-1763, M 1696-1746, B 1696-1735, vestry court minutes 1709-59 & other business 1700-72 **[IR/R 34]**

Dervock: Presbyterian C 1827-31 **[IR/R 34]**

Magheragall: C 1825-35 extracts **[IR/R 31]**

Malone: St John C 1842-87 index, M 1842-4 index **[IR/R 30]**

Shankill *see* **Belfast**

SCHOOLS & UNIVERSITIES
Belfast: *Campbell College Register*, 3rd edn. 1894-1938 **[SCH/CAM]**; 4th edn. 1894-1954 **[SCH/CAM]**. *Methodist College Belfast 1868-1938: a survey and retrospect*, by J.W. Henderson (2 vols. 1939) **[SCH/BEL]**. *Queen's University Belfast Calendar*, 1853, 1922-3, 1939-40, 1944-5 **[UNI/BEL]**. *The history of Royal Belfast Academical Institution 1810-1960*, by J. Jamieson (1959) **[SCH/BEL]**; *List of Students 1810-1912* (1913) **[SCH/BEL]**; *Soane and the Belfast Academical Institution*, by H. Dixon (1976) **[SCH/Tracts]**

ARMAGH

LISTS AND DIRECTORIES
1766 List of families in the parish of Creggan in *Journal of Co. Louth Archaeological Society*, vol. 8, no. 2, 156

1888 *County Armagh one hundred years ago: a guide and directory 1888* by G.H. Bassett (Belfast, 1989) **[IR/D 16]**

LOCAL HISTORY
Maps: Ordnance Survey Maps: *Bessbrook, Crossmaglen & Keady 1906* (reprinted 1987) **[M 171]**. *Armagh county townland maps* (Derry Youth & Community Workshop & Inner City Trust, Mfc, 1989) **[apply to staff]**.

Armagh County & City: *About Armagh in great granny's day and History of the First Presbyterian Church, Armagh*, by G.T. Lundie (Armagh, n.d.) **[IR/L 86]**. *Catalogue* *of manuscripts in the Public Library of Armagh 1928*, by J. Dean (Dundalk, 1928) **[Ireland Tracts 1]**. *Ordnance Survey Memoirs of Ireland*, vol. 1, Parishes of County Armagh 1835-8, ed. A. Day, P. McWilliams, &c (Belfast & Dublin, 1990) **[IR/L 103]**

SCHOOLS
Armagh: *Royal School, Armagh: school register*, ed. M.L. Ferrar (1933) **[SCH/ARM]**

CARLOW

LISTS AND DIRECTORIES
1767 County Carlow Freeholders' List (extracts), in *Irish ancestor*, vol. 12, nos. 1-2 (1980) **[IR/PER]**
1788 *Lucas's General directory of the kingdom of Ireland*, extracts for Carlow, Old Leighlin and Leighlinbridge, in *Irish provincial directories* **[IR/D 1]**; also in *Irish genealogist*, vol. 3, no. 10 (1965) **[IR/PER]**

LOCAL HISTORY
Carlow: *Knights' Fees in counties Wexford, Carlow and Kilkenny (13th-15th century)*, by E.St.J. Brooks (Dublin, 1950) **[IR/L 82]**. *Catherlogiana: Carlow vestries in the olden time [and other papers]* (Carlow Sentinel, 1870-4) **[IR/L 18]**. *The history and antiquities of the county of Carlow*, by J. Ryan (1833) **[MF 3300]**

PARISH REGISTERS
Barragh: (St Paul, Kildavin) CMB 1799-1805, C 1831-79, M 1830-44, B 1838-78 **[IR/R 34]**

SCHOOLS
Carlow: *Carlow College, Knockbeg, Centenary Book (Student Roll 1793-1818)*, ed. P. Macsuibhne (1948) **[SCH/KNO]**

CAVAN

CENSUSES
County: parts of, 1831 and 1841, *Family Tree Maker's family archives census index: Ireland* (CD-ROM) **[Apply to staff]**
Killashandra: part of, 1841 **[MF 1793]**
Munterconnaught, Lurgan & Mullagh: parts of, 1821 **[MF]**

LOCAL HISTORY
Cavan: *General valuation of rateable property for Bailieborough*, 1856 (Dublin, 1856) **[IR/L1]**; *Union of Cavan*, 1857 (Dublin, 1857) **[IR/L 2]**; *Union of Kells, in the counties of Meath and Cavan*, 1854 (Dublin, 1854) **[IR/L 4]**; *Union of Granard*, 1855 (photocopy) **[IR/L 156]**. *Freemen of the borough of Cavan [1697-1838]*, by T.S. Smyth (reprinted from *Breifne*, vol. 1, 1959) **[Ireland Tracts 1]**. *Ordnance Survey Memoirs of Ireland*, vol. 40, Parishes of South Ulster: Cavan, Leitrim, Louth, Monaghan and Sligo, ed. A. Day, P. McWilliams, &c (Belfast & Dublin, 1997) **[IR/L 142]**. 'High sheriffs of counties Cavan and Meath 1714-1823', in *Some Irish lists*, vol. 3 **[IR/G 125]**

CLARE

LISTS AND DIRECTORIES
1768 County Clare voters' & freeholders' list, in *Irish ancestor*, vol. 18, no. 1 (1986) **[IR/PER]**
1788 *Lucas's General directory of the kingdom of Ireland*, extracts for Ennis, in *Corporation book of Ennis* **[IR/L 148]**; also in *Irish provincial directories* **[IR/D 1]**; also in *Irish genealogist*, vol. 4, no. 1 (1968) **[IR/PER]**
1799 Businessmen of Ennis, in *Irish ancestor*, vol. 16, no. 1 (1984) **[IR/PER]**

LOCAL HISTORY
Clare: *Books of survey and distribution, being abstracts of various surveys and instruments of title 1636-1703; vol. 4, County of Clare* (Dublin, 1967) **[Apply to staff]**. 'Justices of the Peace for co. Clare 1661-1862', in *Some Irish lists*, vol. 1 **[IR/G 123]**. 'High sheriffs of co. Clare 1577-1892', in *Some Irish lists*, vol. 2 **[IR/G 124]**
Ennis: *Corporation book of Ennis*, ed. B. O'Dalaigh (Dublin, 1990) **[IR/L 148]**
Scarriff: *General valuation of rateable property in Ireland: Union of Scarriff in the counties of Clare and Galway*, 1855 (Dublin, 1855) **[IR/L 6]**

NEWSPAPERS
Clare Examiner & Limerick Advertiser, Ennis, 1882, and January 1887 to 5 November 1887 **[MF 2532-3]**

CORK

LISTS AND DIRECTORIES
1758 *Clare's brief directory of the city of Cork*, A-K only, in *Irish genealogist*, vol. 1, no. 8 **[IR/PER]**
1766 Notes on inhabitants of Kilmichael, in *Journal of Cork Historical & Archaeological Society*, vol. 26, p. 29 **[IR/PER]**
1769-70 *Clare's brief directory of the city of Cork*, in *Irish genealogist*, vol. 1, no. 8 (1940) **[IR/PER]**
1787 *Lucas's city and county of Cork directory* (1787; reprinted 1965) **[IR/D 1]**
1805-07 *Holden's triennial directory* (4th edn.), vol. 2, includes Cork **[MF 2687 or MX/D 13]**
1805-08 *Holden's triennial directory* (4th edn. including the year 1808), vol. 2, includes Cork **[MX/D 19]**
1842-3 *The city and county of Cork Post Office general directory 1842-3* (reprinted Sydney, 1996) **[IR/D 1842]**
1873 *Street's Indian & Colonial mercantile directory*, includes Cork **[IND/D 13]**
1921 *Purcell's Cork almanac 1921 with city, county & trade directories* **[IR/D 5]**

LOCAL HISTORY
County: *Researching in Cork*, by T. McCarthy **[Audio cassette, 1994]**. *Griffith's Valuation* transcript of co. Cork (Mfc, 1988) **[Apply to staff]**. *Land and the people of 19th-century Cork: the rural economy & the land question*, by J.S. Donnelly (1975) **[Store A]**. *Cork & Kerry families in John Burke's 'The history of the commoners in Great Britain & Ireland (London, 1833)'*, by A.E. Casey (TS, 1963) **[IR/G 196]**. *The Lismore papers: autobiographical notes, remembrances and diaries [of] Sir Richard Boyle, first and 'Great' Earl of Cork, vols. 1-2 (1611-29)*, by A.B. Grosart (TS, 1963) **[IR/G 196]**. *Cork County Library*, by T. Cadogan **[Audio cassette, 1994]**
Bandon: *The history of Bandon*, by G. Bennett (Cork, 1862 **[IR/L 10]**; also Mfc, 1991 **[Apply to staff]**)

21

Buttevant: *Historical and topographical notes etc on Buttevant, Castletownroche, Doneraile, Mallow and places in their vicinity*, by J.G. White (4 vols. 1905-16) [vol 2 missing 1992] **[IR/L 14-17]**

Castlemartyr: *The vestry book of Castlemartyr, co. Cork, 1751-1811*, by John Pratt (MS, 1926) **[IR/L 19]**

Cork: *The council book of the corporation of the city of Cork 1609-1643 & 1690-1800*, by R. Caulfield (Guildford, 1876) **[IR/L 26]**. *Cork Franciscan records 1764-1831*, by W.D. O'Connell (Cork, 1942) **[Ireland Tracts 1]**. City & county of Cork register of freemen admitted 1815-18, in *Journal of Cork historical & archaeological society*, vol. 16 (1910) 168 & vol. 17 (1911) 25 **[IR/PER]**. Chief magistrates of Cork city 1199-1773, in *Some Irish lists*, vol. 2 **[IR/G 124]**. Sheriffs of the city of Cork 1656-1773, in *Some Irish lists*, vol. 3 **[IR/G 125]**

Drishane *see* **Nohovaldaly**

Duhallow Barony: *Index of lands [recorded] in the Registry of Deeds & Leases, Henrietta Street, Dublin, 1708-38*, by A.E. Casey (TS, 1963) **[IR/G 196]**

Fermoy: *St Patrick's Church Fermoy*, by N. Brunicardi (Fermoy Heritage Series, No. 4, 1986) **[Tracts Box]**

Kinsale: *The council book of the corporation of Kinsale 1652-1800*, by R. Caulfield (Guildford, 1879) **[IR/L 59]**. *Short history of Kinsale*, by M. Mulcahy (Kinsale, 1968) **[IR/L 144]**. *St Multose Church, Kinsale*, by J.L. Darling (Cork, 1895) **[Ireland Tracts 1]**

Nohovaldaly: *Extracts of land records of East Nohovaldaly, 1690-1830*, by M. Daly (TS, 1963) **[IR/G 196]**. *Heads of families in Tithe Applotment Books, parishes of Drishane (1832) and Nohovaldaly (1834)*, by A.E. Casey (TS, 1963) **[IR/G 196]**

Youghal: *The council book of the corporation of Youghal 1610-1659, 1666-1687 & 1690-1800*, by R. Caulfield (Guildford, 1878) **[IR/L 83]**. *St Mary's collegiate church, Youghal, co. Cork, a brief outline of its history*, by V. Darling (1929) **[Ireland Tracts 1]**. Borough of Youghal list of marksmen 1837, in *Irish records: sources for family & local history*, p.76 **[Apply to staff]**

MONUMENTAL INSCRIPTIONS

Aghinagh: burial ground **[IR/M 25]**
Ballingeary: church **[IR/G 196]**
Ballycurrany: burial ground **[IR/M 25]**
Ballydesmond *see* **Nohovaldaly**
Ballyvourney: church, St Gobnait's Old & New cemeteries **[IR/G 196]**; *see also* **Coolea**
Boherbue & Kiskeam: RC cemeteries **[IR/G 196]**
Carrigrohanebeg: burial ground **[IR/M 25]**
Castlemagner: Protestant church, RC & Protestant churchyards, & cemetery **[IR/G 196]**
Clondrohid: cemetery **[IR/G 196]**
Clonfert: cemetery & Newmarket cemetery **[IR/G 196]**
Clonmult: burial ground **[IR/M 25]**
Coolea: church **[IR/G 196]**
Cullen: RC cemetery **[IR/G 196]**
Dangandonovan: burial ground **[IR/M 25]**
Desertmore: burial ground **[IR/M 25]**
Drishane *see* **Millstreet**
Dromagh: Protestant & RC cemeteries **[IR/G 196]**
Dromtariffe: cemetery **[IR/G 196]**; *see also* **Dromagh**
Dunderrow: burial ground **[IR/M 25]**
Gongane Barra: cemetery **[IR/G 196]**
Inchigeela: church, churchyard, Old & New Cemeteries **[IR/G 196]**; *see also* **Gongane**

Barra and Ballingeary
Kilcrea: burial ground **[IR/M 25]**
Killeagh: burial ground **[IR/M 25]**
Kilmeen *see* **Boherbue & Kiskeam** and **Kiskeam**
Kilnaglory: burial ground **[IR/M 25]**
Kilnamartyra: church, churchyard & Old Cemetery **[IR/G 196]**
Kinsale: church, in *St Multose Church, Kinsale*, by J.L. Darling **[Ireland Tracts 1]**
Kiskeam: cemetery **[IR/G 196]**; *see also* **Boherbue**
Knocknagree *see* **Nohovaldaly**
Millstreet: Old & New cemeteries, Church of Ireland churchyard, RC churchyard, Drishane
     cemetery **[IR/G 196]**
Mologga: churchyard, in *Irish genealogist*, vol. 2, no. 12 (1955) 390-3 **[IR/PER]**
Newmarket *see* **Clonfert**
Nohoval *see* **Nohovaldaly**
Nohovaldaly: Nohoval graveyard, Ballydesmond cemetery, Knocknagree cemetery **[IR/G
     196]**
Tisaxon: burial ground **[IR/M 25]**
Titeskin: burial ground **[IR/M 25]**
Youghal: church, in *Topographer and genealogist*, vol. 2 (1853) 194-207 **[PER/TOP]**

NEWSPAPERS
Weekly Star & General Advertiser, Cork, 1867 **[MF 2568]**
*Index to Cork Herald or The Munster Advertiser (later The Cork Advertiser) May 1786 to
     November 1800* (MS, n.d.) **[IR/L 168]**
A collection of abstracts from newspapers printed in Cork City, 1753-71, 1782-84 (includes
     marriage & death notices), by J.T. Collins (TS, 1963) **[IR/G 196]**

PARISH REGISTERS
Ballymodan: St Peter C 1695-1863 extracts, M 1695-1845 extracts, B 1695-1878 extracts
     [IR/R 31]
Ballyvourney *see* **Muskerry West**
Fermoy: Garrison Church C 1920-22 **[IR/R 34]**
Inchigeelagh *see* **Muskerry West**
Kilbrogan: C 1752-1872, M 1753-1863, B 1707-1877 **[IR/R 31]**.
Kilmichael *see* **Muskerry West**
Kilnamartery *see* **Muskerry West**
Muskerry West, Barony: Births 1864-5 and M 1864-1900 from Registrar General's Office
     (TS, 1963) **[IR/G 196]**

PERIODICALS
Cork Historical & Archaeological Society journal, vols. 1-43 (1892-1938) **[IR/PER]**

SCHOOLS
Knocknagree: *Knocknagree National School: list of teachers 1840-1962*, by M. Daly (TS,
     1963) **[IR/G 196, pp 2044-8]**

DERRY *formerly* LONDONDERRY

CENSUSES
County: *Index to the county Londonderry 1831 census* (Londonderry, Mfc, 1989) **[Apply to
     staff]**; also MF (1995) **[MF 1789-93]**. Also parts of 1831 and 1841, *Family Tree
     Maker's family archives census index: Ireland* (CD-ROM) **[Apply to staff]**

LISTS AND DIRECTORIES
1803 List of families of ... parish of Faughanville, in *Ulster Genealogical & Historical Guild Newsletter,* vol. 1, no. 10 **[IR/PER]**
1908 *Sentinel's Derry almanac, north-west directory & grand advertiser for 1908* (Mfc, 1995) **[Apply to staff]**

LOCAL HISTORY
Derry County & City: *Griffith's Valuation* index and copy of co. Londonderry (Mfc, 1979) **[Apply to staff]**. *Londonderry and the London Companies 1609-1629, being a survey and other documents submitted to King Charles I*, by Sir Thomas Phillips (Belfast, 1928) **[IR/L 92]**. *A particular of the howses and famylyes in London Derry, May 15 1628*, by R.G.S. King (1936) **[IR/L 65]**. *The surnames of Derry*, by B. Mitchell (1992) **[IR/L 171]**. *The Civil Survey, 1654-1656; vol. 3, counties of Londonderry, Donegal & Tyrone*, by R.C. Simington (Dublin, 1937) **[IR/G 17]**. *A true account of the siege of London-Derry*, by G. Walker (London, 1689; reprinted 1907) **[IR/L 30]**. *The Londonderry journal & general advertiser: a local index: vol. 1, 1772-1775*, ed. C. Holmes (Londonderry, 1988) **[IR/L 98]**. *The first and second valuations of the city of Derry: 1832 and 1858*, by Derry Youth and Community Workshop (Londonderry, 1984) **[Enquiry Desk, Shelf 9]**. *Fighters of Derry: their deeds and descendants*, by W.R. Young (1932) **[IR/L 28]**. *St Columbs' Cathedral, Londonderry, historical guide*, by R.G.S. King (1952) **[IR/L 66]**. *Historic gleanings from county Derry (and some from Fermanagh): traditions, superstitions and legends*, by S. Martin (Dublin, 1955) **[IR/L 29]**. *Ordnance Survey Memoirs of Ireland*, ed. A. Day, P. McWilliams, &c.; vol. 6, Parishes of County Londonderry I 1830, 1834, 1836: Arboe, Artrea, Ballinderry, Ballyscullion, Magherafelt, Termoneeny (Belfast & Dublin, 1990) **[IR/L 108]**; vol. 9, Londonderry II 1833-5: Roe Valley Central (1991) **[IR/L 111]**; vol. 11, Londonderry III 1831-5: Roe Valley Lower (1991) **[IR/L 113]**; vol. 15, Londonderry IV 1824, 1833-5: Roe Valley Upper: Dungiven (1992) **[IR/L 117]**; vol. 18, Londonderry V 1830, 1833, 1836-7: Maghera & Tamlacht O'Crilly (1993) **[IR/L 120]**; vol. 22, Londonderry VI 1831, 1833, 1835-6: North-East Londonderry (1993) **[IR/L 124]**; vol. 25, Londonderry VII 1834-5: North West Londonderry (1994) **[IR/L 127]**; vol. 27, Londonderry VIII 1830, 1833-7, 1839: East Londonderry (1994) **[IR/L 129]**; vol. 28, Londonderry IX 1832-8: West Londonderry (1995) **[IR/L 130]**; vol. 30, Londonderry X 1830, 1833-5, 1838: mid-Londonderry (1995) **[IR/L 132]**; vol. 31, Londonderry XI 1821, 1833, 1836-7: South Londonderry (1995) **[IR/L 133]**; vol. 33, Londonderry XII 1829-30, 1832, 1834-36: Coleraine and Mouth of the Bann (1995) **[IR/L 135]**; vol. 34, Londonderry XIII 1831-8: Clondermot and the Waterside (1996) **[IR/L 136]**; vol. 36, Londonderry XIV 1833-4, 1836, 1838: Faughanvale (1996) **[IR/L 138]**
Banagher: Protestant householders, 1740 & 1766, in *Some Irish lists*, vol. 2 **[IR/G 124]**
Edenderry: *The parish of Edenderry*, by H.I. Law (Omagh, 1949) **[IR/L 43]**
Faughanvale: Protestant householders, 1740, in *Some Irish lists*, vol. 2 **[IR/G 124]**

MONUMENTAL INSCRIPTIONS
Aghanloo: Old Churchyard & Church of Ireland churchyard, in *Family links*, vol. 2, no. 3 (1985) 15-16 **[IR/PER]**; New Church & (extracts) Old Churchyard, in *Historic gleanings from county Derry* by S. Martin (1955) 42-45 **[IR/L 29]**
Ballykelly: churchyard burial ground half mile north of village, Presbyterian burial ground, St Finlough's RC graveyard, in *Family links*, vol. 2, no. 3 (1985) 16-19 and no. 4 (1985) 12-19 **[IR/PER]**
Balteagh: churchyard and Presbyterian burial ground, in *Family links*, vol. 2, no. 4 (1985) 20-1 **[IR/PER]**

Camus Juxta Bann: churchyard, in *Scottish genealogist*, vol. 11, no. 2 (1964) 6-28 **[IR/PER]**

Derramore: Presbyterian graveyard, in *Family links*, vol. 2, no. 4 (1985) 21 **[IR/PER]**

Drumachose: Old Churchyard & Presbyterian graveyard, in *Family links*, vol. 2, no. 4 (1985) 21-22, and no. 5 (1985) 19-20 **[IR/PER]**

Edenderry: church, in *The parish of Edenderry* by H.I. Law (1949) 23-27 **[IR/L 43]**

Largy: Presbyterian graveyard, in *Family links*, vol. 2, no. 5 (1985) 20-21 **[IR/PER]**

Limavady: First Presbyterian graveyard, Reformed Presbyterian graveyard, RC graveyard, in *Family links*, vol. 2, no. 5 (1985) 21-24; no. 6 (1986) 19-20 **[IR/PER]**

Macosquin *see* **Camus Juxta Ban**

Magilligan: Presbyterian graveyard, RC graveyard, in *Family links*, vol. 2, no. 6 (1986) 20-22 **[IR/PER]**

Myroe: Presbyterian Church, in *Family links*, vol. 2, no. 6 (1986) 22-23 **[IR/PER]**

Tamlaghfinlagan: in *Family links*, vol. 2, no. 4 (1985) 12-13 **[IR/PER]**

Tamlaght: churchyard, in *Family links*, vol. 2, no. 4 (1985), 12-13 **[IR/PER]**

Tamlaghtard: in *Family links*, vol. 2, no. 6 (1986) 23-24 **[IR/PER]**

NEWSPAPERS

The Londonderry Journal and General Advertiser: a local index, 1772-1775, by C. Holmes (Londonderry, 1988) **[IR/L 98]**

PARISH REGISTERS

Aghadowey: C 1845-86, M 1845-90 (for families A-Knox only), in *Irish Family links*, vols. 2-3 (1987-9) **[IR/PER]**.

Derry: Cathedral, Templemore (St Columb) 1642-1703 **[IR/R 12]**.

Drumachose: C 1857-68 extracts, B 1855-74 extracts **[IR/R 31]**

SCHOOLS

Caw: Foyle College Register 1847-1853 **[SCH/Tracts]**. *Scholars from Foyle College at Trinity College, Dublin* **[SCH/Tracts]**. *Foyle College Times (Our School Times)*, various **[SCH/FOY]**

Londonderry: *Londonderry Free Grammar School Register 1617-1814*, ed. M. Springham **[SCH/Tracts]**

Magee: *Magee Presbyterian College Calendar 1892-3* **[UNI/MAG]**

DONEGAL

LISTS AND DIRECTORIES

1824 *Pigot & Co's Directory*, extract for Pettigo, in *North Irish roots*, vol. 3, no. 1 **[IR/PER]**

1848 *'Armagh Guardian' handbook or directory for county of Fermanagh*, extract for Pettigo, in *North Irish roots*, vol. 3, no. 1 **[IR/PER]**

LOCAL HISTORY

Donegal: *A guide to tracing your Donegal ancestors*, by G.F. Duffy (1996) **[IR/L 172]**. *Griffith's Valuation* transcript of co. Donegal (Mfc, 1987) **[Apply to staff]**. *The Civil Survey 1654-1656; vol. 3, Counties of Donegal, Londonderry & Tyrone*, by R.C. Simington (Dublin, 1937) **[IR/G 17]**. *Ordnance Survey Memoirs of Ireland*, vol. 38, Parishes of County Donegal I: 1833-5: North-East Donegal, ed. A. Day, P. McWilliams, &c (Belfast & Dublin, 1997) **[IR/L 140]**; vol. 39, Donegal II: 1835-6: Mid, West and South Donegal (1997) **[IR/L 141]**. *Donegal tithe applotment books: Lower & Upper Fahan, Muff, Inch, Burt, Templecrone, Lettermacaward, Inishkeel, All Saints, Leck, Raymaghy, Taughboyne, Killea, Raphoe, Clonleigh, Convoy,*

Stranorlar, Donaghmore (MF, 1997) **[MF 3479 and 3480]**. 'High sheriffs of co. Donegal 1607-1814', in *Some Irish lists*, vol. 2 **[IR/G 124]**

Glendermot: 'Householders of Glendermot, co. Donegal, 1663 & 1740', in *Some Irish lists*, vol. 2 **[IR/G 124]**

Mevagh: *Mevagh down the years*, by L.W. Lucas (Belfast, 1962) **[IR/L 68]**

MONUMENTAL INSCRIPTIONS

Ballyshannon: churchyard, in *Family links*, vol. 1, no. 3 (1981) 13-14, and no. 4 (1982) 31-4 **[IR/PER]**

DOWN

LISTS AND DIRECTORIES

1824 *Pigot & Co's Directory*, extract for Killyleagh/Killileigh, in *North Irish roots*, vol. 4, no. 1 **[IR/PER]**

1837 Lewis's Topographical directory of ... Hilltown, in *North Irish roots*, vol. 4, no. 1 **[IR/PER]**

1843 Wilson's Post Office directory of ... Ardglass, in *North Irish roots*, vol. 4, no. 1 **[IR/PER]**

1886 *County Down one hundred years ago: a guide and directory 1886*, by G.H. Bassett (Belfast, 1988) **[IR/D 17]**

LOCAL HISTORY

Maps: Ordnance Survey Maps: *Bangor (East) 1901* (reprinted 1995) **[M 841]**; *Bangor (West) 1901* (reprinted 1995) **[M 842]**; *Comber & Saintfield 1904* (reprinted 1992) **[M 614]**; *Donaghadee 1901* (reprinted 1995) **[M 819]**; *Downpatrick 1901* (reprinted 1986) **[M 155]**; *Newtownards 1901* (reprinted 1995) **[M 825]**

County: *Two centuries of life in Down 1600-1800*, by J. Stevenson (Belfast, 1920) **[IR/L 35]**. Ordnance Survey Memoirs of Ireland, ed. A. Day, P. McWilliams, &c.; vol. 3, Parishes of County Down I 1834-6: South Down (Belfast & Dublin, 1990) **[IR/L 105]**; vol. 7, Down II 1832-4, 1837: North Down (1991) **[IR/L 109]**; vol. 12, Down III 1833-8: Mid Down (1992) **[IR/L 114]**; vol. 17, Down IV 1833-7: East Down & Lecale (1992) **[IR/L 119]**. *The Hamilton manuscripts: containing some account of the settlement of the territories of the Upper Clandeboye, Great Ardes, and Dufferin, in the County of Down*, by Sir James Hamilton, Knight, ed. T.K.Lowry (Belfast, 1867) **[IR/G 30]**

Banbridge: *Two centuries of profit and pleasure in Union Band Masonic Lodge No 336, Banbridge, 1759-1959*, by R.J. Given (Newry, 1959) **[IR/L 143]**

Donaghcloney: *An Ulster parish, being a history of Donaghcloney, Waringstown*, by E.D. Atkinson (Dublin, 1898) **[IR/L 33]**

Down: *The cathedral church of Down, Downpatrick: brief history and guide* (n.d.) **[Ireland Tracts 1]**

Newmills: *Newmills congregation 1796-1947: historical sketch*, by J. Nimmons (Lurgan, 1948) **[IR/L 70]**

Newry: *A history of Nelson Masonic Lodge No 18 Newry*, by F.C. Crossle (Newry, 1909) **[IR/L 71]**

MONUMENTAL INSCRIPTIONS

Aghlisnafin: RC graveyard **[IR/M 18]**

Annahilt: graveyard, Presbyterian graveyard **[IR/M 21]**

Ardglass: graveyard **[IR/M 18]**

Ardkeen: graveyard, Church of Ireland church **[IR/M 19]**; graveyard, Church of Ireland church **[IR/M 27]**

Ardquin: graveyard **[IR/M 19]**; graveyard **[IR/M 27]**

Baileysmill: Reformed Presbyterian graveyard **[IR/M 17]**
Ballee: graveyard, Non-Subscribing Presbyterian graveyard **[IR/M 18]**
Balligan: graveyard **[IR/M 20]**
Balloo House Mausoleum **[IR/M 20]**
Ballooly: RC graveyard **[IR/M 22]**
Ballyblack: Presbyterian graveyard **[IR/M 19]**
Ballycarn: Presbyterian graveyard **[IR/M 17]**
Ballycopeland: Presbyterian **[IR/M 20]**
Ballycranbeg: RC graveyard **[IR/M 19]**; RC graveyard **[IR/M 27]**
Ballycruttle: RC graveyard **[IR/M 18]**
Ballyculter: graveyard **[IR/M 18]**
Ballydown: Presbyterian graveyard **[IR/M 28]**
Ballygalget: RC graveyard **[IR/M 19]**; RC graveyard **[IR/M 27]**
Ballygilbert: Presbyterian church **[IR/M 20]**
Ballygowan: graveyard **[IR/M 18]**
Ballyhalbert: graveyard & Church of Ireland **[IR/M 20]**
Ballyhemlin: Non-Subscribing Presbyterian **[IR/M 20]**
Ballykinler: RC graveyard **[IR/M 18]**
Ballymacashen: Reformed Presbyterian graveyard **[IR/M 18]**
Ballymageogh: RC graveyard **[IR/M 19]**
Ballymartin: RC graveyard **[IR/M 19]**
Ballynahinch: First Presbyterian graveyard, Second Presbyterian graveyard **[IR/M 18]**
Ballyphilip: graveyard, Portaferry & Church of Ireland graveyard **[IR/M 19]**; graveyard, Portaferry & Church of Ireland graveyard **[IR/M 27]**
Ballytrustan: graveyard **[IR/M 19]**, graveyard **[IR/M 27]**
Ballywalter: Whitechurch graveyard **[IR/M 20]**
Banbridge: Cemetery, Crozier Monument, Downshire Road non-subscribing Presbyterian Church, First Presbyterian graveyard, Roman Catholic graveyard, Scarva Street Presbyterian graveyard **[IR/M 28]**
Bangor: Abbey graveyard **[IR/M 20]**; Bangor Church of Ireland church **[IR/M 20]**; Bangor First Presbyterian church **[IR/M 20]**; Castle Park, Bangor **[IR/M 20]**
Blaris: graveyard **[IR/M 18]**
Boardmills: First & Second Presbyterian graveyard **[IR/M 17]**
Breda: graveyard **[IR/M 17]**, addenda **[IR/M 19]** and **[IR/M 27]**
Bright: graveyard **[IR/M 18]**
Cargacreevy: Presbyterian graveyard **[IR/M 21]**
Carrowdore: graveyard **[IR/M 20]**
Carryduff: Presbyterian graveyard **[IR/M 17]**, addenda **[IR/M 21]**
Castlereagh: Presbyterian graveyard **[IR/M 17]**, addenda **[IR/M 21]**
Clandeboys House [IR/M 20]
Clare: RC graveyard **[IR/M 28]**
Cloghy: Presbyterian **[IR/M 20]**
Clough: Presbyterian graveyard, Non-Subscribing Presbyterian graveyard **[IR/M 18]**
Comber: **graveyard [IR/M 18], addenda [IR/M 19] and [IR/M 27]**; Gillespie Monument **[IR/M 18]**
Conlig: Presbyterian church **[IR/M 20]**
Copeland Island: cemetery **[MF 693]**; graveyard **[IR/M 20]**
Donaghadee: graveyard **[IR/M 20]**
Donaghcloney: graveyard, Presbyterian graveyard **[IR/M 22]**; Old churchyard, in *An Ulster Parish: being a history of Donaghcloney (Waringstown)*, by E.D. Atkinson (1898) 125-9 **[IR/L 33]**
Downpatrick: Cathedral graveyard, Church of Ireland graveyard, Non-Subscribing

Presbyterian graveyard, Presbyterian graveyard, RC graveyard **[IR/M 18]**; Cathedral graveyard, Church of Ireland graveyard, Non-Subscribing Presbyterian graveyard, Presbyterian graveyard, St Patrick's RC Cemetery, St Patrick's RC church graveyard **[IR/M 32]**

Dromara: graveyard, First Presbyterian graveyard, Second Presbyterian graveyard, Reformed Presbyterian graveyard **[IR/M 22]**

Dromore: Cathedral, First Presbyterian graveyard, Second Presbyterian graveyard, Non-Subscribing Presbyterian graveyard, RC graveyard **[IR/M 22]**

Drumaroad: RC graveyard **[IR/M 18]**

Drumbeg: graveyard **[IR/M 17]**, addenda **[IR/M 18]**

Drumbo: Church of Ireland graveyard & Presbyterian graveyard **[IR/M 17]** and **[IR/M 18]**; graveyard addenda **[IR/M 21]**

Drumlough: Presbyterian graveyard **[IR/M 22]**

Dundonald: graveyard **[IR/M 17]**

Dunsfort: graveyard, RC graveyard **[IR/M 18]**

Edenderry House graveyard **[IR/M 17]**

Eglantine: Church of Ireland graveyard **[IR/M 21]**

Finnis: RC graveyard **[IR/M 22]**

Garvaghy: graveyard, Presbyterian graveyard **[IR/M 22]**

Gilnahirk: Presbyterian graveyard **[IR/M 21]**

Glasdrumman: RC graveyard **[IR/M 19]**

Glastry: Presbyterian graveyard **[IR/M 20]**

Gransha: Presbyterian graveyard **[IR/M 17]**

Grey Abbey grounds & graveyard **[IR/M 19]**

Groomsport: Church of Ireland church **[IR/M 20]**; Presbyterian church **[IR/M 20]**

Hillhall: Presbyterian graveyard **[IR/M 17]**

Hillsborough: graveyard, Society of Friends graveyard, Hill Monument **[IR/M 21]**

Holywood: graveyard **[IR/M 17]** and **[IR/M 18]**

Inch: graveyard **[IR/M 18]** and **[IR/M 32]**

Inishargy: graveyard **[IR/M 20]**

Kilcarn: graveyard **[IR/M 18]**

Kilclief: graveyard, RC graveyard **[IR/M 18]**

Kilhorne: Church of Ireland graveyard **[IR/M 19]**

Kilkeel: Old Graveyard, Church of Ireland graveyard, Moravian graveyard **[IR/M 19]**

Kilkinamurry: Presbyterian graveyard **[IR/M 22]**

Killaney: graveyard & Presbyterian graveyard **[IR/M 17]**

Killaresy: graveyard **[IR/M 18]**

Killinakin: graveyard **[IR/M 18]**

Killinchy: Non-Subscribing Presbyterian graveyard **[IR/M 18]**

Killough: graveyard, Presbyterian graveyard **[IR/M 18]**

Killybawn: graveyard, and addenda **[IR/M 17]**

Killyleagh: Old Graveyard, Church of Ireland graveyard, Presbyterian graveyard **[IR/M 18]**; Presbyterian graveyard **[IR/M 32]**

Killysuggan: graveyard **[IR/M 18]**

Kilmegan: graveyard **[IR/M 18]**

Kilmood: graveyard **[IR/M 18]**

Kilmore: graveyard, Presbyterian graveyard **[IR/M 17]**; graveyard addenda **[IR/M 19]**; graveyard corrigenda & Church of Ireland graveyard corrigenda **[IR/M 27]**

Kilwarlin: Church of Ireland graveyard, Moravian graveyard, RC graveyard **[IR/M 21]**

Kircubbin: graveyard, Presbyterian graveyard **[IR/M 19]**

Knock: graveyard **[IR/M 17]**, addenda **[IR/M 19]**, addenda [IR/M 27]

Knockbreckan: Reformed Presbyterian graveyard **[IR/M 17]**, addenda **[IR/M 21]**

Knockbreda: graveyard [IR/M 17]
Lawrencetown: Roman Catholic graveyard [IR/M 28]
Legacurry: Presbyterian graveyard [IR/M 17]
Lisbane: RC graveyard [IR/M 19]; RC graveyard [IR/M 27]
Lisburn: Cathedral Churchyard [MF 695]
Loughaghery: Presbyterian graveyard [IR/M 21]
Loughinisland: graveyard [IR/M 18] and addenda [IR/M 19]
Lurganville: RC graveyard [IR/M 21]
Magheradrool: graveyard, Church of Ireland graveyard [IR/M 18]; graveyard addenda [IR/M 19]
Magherahamlet: graveyard, Presbyterian graveyard [IR/M 18]
Magheralin: Old Graveyard, Church of Ireland graveyard [IR/M 22]
Magherally: graveyard, Presbyterian graveyard [IR/M 28]
Maze: Presbyterian graveyard [IR/M 21]
Millisle: Presbyterian graveyard [IR/M 20]
Moira: graveyard, Non-Subscribing Presbyterian graveyard, Presbyterian graveyard [IR/M 21]
Moneyrea: Presbyterian graveyard [IR/M 17]
Mourne: Abbey graveyard, Presbyterian graveyard [IR/M 19]
Movilla graveyard, Newtownards [IR/M 19]
Moyallon: Friends' graveyard [IR/M 28]
Newtownards: Church of Ireland graveyard, Priory graveyard [IR/M 19]; *see also* **Movilla**
Old Court Chapel, Strangford [IR/M 18]
Portaferry: RC graveyard [IR/M 19]; RC graveyard [IR/M 27]
Rademan: Non-Subscribing Presbyterian graveyard [IR/M 17]
Raffrey: Presbyterian graveyard [IR/M 18]
Rathmullan: graveyard [IR/M 18]
Ravarra: Non-Subscribing Presbyterian graveyard [IR/M 18]
Rossglass: RC graveyard [IR/M 18]
Saintfield: Church of Ireland graveyard, First Presbyterian graveyard, Second Presbyterian graveyard [IR/M 17]
Saul: RC graveyard [IR/M 18]; graveyard [IR/M 32]
Seaforde: graveyard [IR/M 18]
Seapatrick: graveyard, Church of Ireland church [IR/M 28]
Slanes: graveyard [IR/M 20]
Strangford: *see* Old Court Chapel [IR/M 18]
Tamlaght: graveyard [IR/M 19]
Templepatrick: graveyard [IR/M 20]
Tullymacnous: gravestone [IR/M 18]
Tullylish: graveyard & Presbyterian graveyard [IR/M 28]
Tullynakill: graveyard [IR/M 17] and addenda [IR/M 18]
Waringstown: graveyard, Presbyterian graveyard [IR/M 22]; *see also* Donaghcloney
Whitechurch graveyard, Ballywalter [IR/M 20]

NEWSPAPERS
County Down Spectator. Index to the County Down Spectator & Ulster Standard 1904-1964, by J. McCoy (TS, 1983) **[IR/L 145]**
Downpatrick Recorder. Index to the Downpatrick Recorder 1836-1886, by J. McCoy (1987) **[IR/L 141]**
Newry Magazine: marriage and death notices 1817-1819, in *Some Irish lists*, vol. 6 **[IR/G 128]**
Newtownards Chronicle: Index to the Newtownards Chronicle 1873-1900 & the

Newtownards Independent 1871-1873, by K. Robinson (TS, 1990) **[IR/L 142]**. *Index to the Newtownards Chronicle 1901-39*, by K. Robinson (1995) **[IR/L 142a]**
Newtownards Independent see Newtownards Chronicle
Northern Herald: An index to county Down and Lisburn items in the Northern Herald 1833-36 and in The Northern Star 1792-7, by J. Macoy (1992) **[IR/L 163-4]**
Northern Star see Northern Herald
Ulster Standard see County Down Spectator

PARISH REGISTERS
Banbridge: Presbyterian M 1756-94 **[IR/R 34]**
Kilkeel: C 1816-42, MB 1816-27 **[IR/R 28]**.
Loughin Island: 1760-1806, C 1816-37, M 1815-94, B 1823-38 **[IR/R 31]**
Newry: Presbyterian C 1779-96 & 1809-22, M 1781-97 & 1820-29, in *Irish ancestor*, vols. 11 (1979) & 13 (1981) **[IR/PER]**

PERIODICALS
Banbridge & District Historical Society journal, vols. 1-2 (1989-90) **[IR/PER]**

SCHOOLS
Dundonell: *A history of Cabin Hill 1785-1979: a house, a school and its people*, ed. A.M. Wilson (1979) **[SCH/CAB]**

DUBLIN

LISTS AND DIRECTORIES
1660   Gentlemen resident in co. Dublin in 1660, in *Some Irish lists*, vol. 4 **[IR/G 126]**
1663-8 Residents & property owners in southern co. Dublin 1663-8, in *Some Irish lists*, vol. 4 **[IR/G 126]**
1664   Residents in co. Dublin 1664 (Hearth Tax), in *Some Irish lists*, vol. 7 **[IR/G 129]**
1664   *A list of residents in county of Dublin in 1664*, by G.S. Cary (TS, 1948) **[IR/L 41]**
1684   Clark's List of the principal inhabitants of the City of Dublin, in *Irish genealogist*, vol. 8, no. 1 (1990) **[IR/PER]**
1761, 1762, 1764, 1765, *Wilson's Dublin directory*, in *The gentleman's almanack* **[ALM]**
1766   List of several families in parish of Monkstown, in Register of the Union of Monks Town **[IR/R 26]**
1767, 1768, 1769, 1770, 1773, 1774, 1775, 1776, 1777 **[Apply to staff]**, 1778, 1780, 1781 **[Apply to staff]**, 1782, 1783, 1784, 1785, 1786, 1787, 1788, *Wilson's Dublin directory*, in *The gentleman's almanack* **[ALM]**
1788   Proprietors of private sedan chairs in Dublin, 25 Mch 1788, in *Some Irish lists*, vol. 7 **[IR/G 129]**
1789 **[Apply to staff]**, 1790, 1791, *Wilson's Dublin directory*, in *The gentleman's almanack* **[ALM]**
1791   *Wilson's Dublin directory*, merchants & traders A-Ben only, in *British Columbia genealogist*, vol. 2, nos. 1-2 **[CAN/BC/PER]**
1792   *Wilson's Dublin directory*, in *The gentleman's almanack* **[ALM]**
1793, 1795, 1796, 1797, 1798, 1799, 1800, 1801, 1802, 1803, 1804, 1805, *Wilson's Dublin directory*, in *The treble almanack* **[ALM]**
1805-07 *Holden's Triennial directory* (4th edn.), vol. 2, includes Dublin **[MF 2687 or MX/D 13]**
1805-08 *Holden's Triennial directory* (4th edn. including the year 1808), vol. 2, includes Dublin **[MX/D 19]**
1806, 1807, 1808, 1809, 1810, 1811 **[also Mfc, apply to staff]**, 1812, 1814, 1815 **[also**

Mfc, apply to staff], 1816, 1817, 1818, 1819, 1820, 1821, 1822, 1823, *Wilson's Dublin directory,* in *The treble almanack* **[ALM]**
1824   *Pigot & Co's City of Dublin and Hibernian provincial directory* (London, 1824) **[Enquiry Desk, Shelf 7]**
1824, 1825, 1826, 1827, 1828, 1829 **[also Mfc, apply to staff]**, 1830, 1831 *Wilson's Dublin directory,* in *The treble almanack* **[ALM]**
1832   *Watson's or the gentleman's & citizens almanack [including] the Post Office annual directory for 1832: containing an alphabetical list of the nobility, gentry, merchants & others in Dublin & vicinity* (Mfc, 1992) **[Apply to staff]**
1832, 1833, 1834, *Folds's Post Office annual directory* [for Dublin], in *The treble almanack* **[ALM]**
1835   *Pettigrew & Oulton's Dublin almanac & general register of Ireland,* with *Pettigrew & Oulton's Dublin directory* **[ALM]**
1835   *Wilson's Dublin directory,* in *The treble almanack* **[ALM]**
1837, 1838, *Folds's Post Office annual directory* [for Dublin], in *The treble almanack* **[ALM]**
1840   *Pettigrew & Oulton's Dublin almanac & general register of Ireland,* with *Pettigrew & Oulton's Dublin directory* **[ALM]**
1842   *Pettigrew & Oulton's Dublin Directory* **[Mfc, apply to staff]**
1845, 1846, *Pettigrew & Oulton's Dublin almanac & general register of Ireland,* with *Pettigrew & Oulton's Dublin directory* **[ALM]**
1849   *Thom's Irish almanack & official directory,* with the *Post Office Dublin city and county directory* **[Apply to staff]**
1850   *The Dublin pictorial guide and directory for 1850* **[IR/D 1850]**
1852   *Thom's Irish almanack & official directory,* with the *Post Office Dublin city and county directory* **[IR/D 1852]**
1868   *Thom's ... Post Office Dublin city & county directory* **[Mfc, apply to staff]**
1873   *Street's Indian and colonial mercantile directory,* includes Dublin **[IND/D 13]**
1877   *Pilkington's Post Office Dublin directory and calendar* **[IR/D 2]**
1877   *Thom's ... Post Office Dublin city & county directory* **[Mfc, apply to staff]**
1899   *The Post Office Dublin directory & calendar for 1899* **[IR/D 1899]**
1904   *Thom's Post Office Dublin directory and calendar* **[IR/D 4]**
1908   *Thom's ... Post Office Dublin city & county directory* **[IR/D 1908]**
1909   *Thom's ... Post Office Dublin city & county directory* **[Apply to staff]**
1939   *Thom's Post Office Dublin directory and calendar* **[IR/D 14]**
1974   *Thom's Dublin & county street directory* **[IR/D 9]**

LOCAL HISTORY
Maps: Ordnance Survey Maps: *Dublin: The Castle 1843* (reprinted 1988) **[M 304]**
Dublin County & City: *A guide to tracing your Dublin ancestors,* by J.G. Ryan (Dublin, 1988) **[IR/L 100]**. *Griffith's Valuation* index and copy of City of Dublin (Mfc, 1986) **[Apply to staff]**. 'An alphabetical list of the freemen of the city of Dublin Jan 1774-Jan 1824' in *Irish ancestor,* vol. 15 (1983), nos. 1 & 2 **[IR/PER]**. *The Civil Survey 1654-1656; vol. 7, County of Dublin,* by R.C. Simington (Dublin, 1945) **[IR/G 21]**. *The history and antiquities of the city of Dublin,* by W. Harris (1766, reprinted 1994) **[IR/L 173]**. *Directory of historic Dublin guilds,* by M. Clark & R. Refausse (1993) **[IR/L 162]**. *Dublin hanged: crime, law enforcement and punishment in late 18th-century Dublin,* by B. Henry (1994) **[IR/L 169]**. *Register of the hospital of St John the Baptist without the New Gate, Dublin,* by E.St.J. Brooks (Irish Manuscripts Commission, 1936) **[IR/L 39]**. *Primatus Dublinienses or the primacy of the see of Dublin* by P. Talbot ed. W.E. Kenny (Dublin, 1947) **[IR/G 152]**. *St Bartholomew's: a history of the Dublin parish,* by K. Milne (Dublin, 1963) **[IR/L 40]**. *The Dublin city 'Roll of Quakers'* reconstructed by M. Clark in *Irish genealogist,* vol. 7, no. 4 (1989)

[IR/PER]. *St John's Monkstown: the story of an Irish church*, by R.W. Harden (Dublin, 1911) **[IR/L 69]**. *Court book of the liberty of St Sepulchre within the jurisdiction of the archbishop of Dublin 1586-90* ed., by H. Wood (Dublin, 1930) **[IR/L 153]**. *Dublin: a study in environment*, by J. Harvey (London, 1949) **[IR/L 38]**. *Dublin: civic week handbook 1929* (Dublin, 1929) **[IR/L 37]**. *Southern Fingal, being the 6th part of a history of county Dublin*, by F.E. Ball (Dublin, 1920) **[IR/L 90]**. High sheriffs of co. Dublin 1300-1836, in *Some Irish lists*, vol. 2 **[IR/G 124]**. Chief magistrates of Dublin city 1308-1881, in *Some Irish lists*, vol. 2 **[IR/G 124]**. Bailiffs & sheriffs of Dublin city 1308-1884, in *Some Irish lists*, vol. 3 **[IR/G 125]**. Church wardens of Crumlin, co. Dublin 1757-1830, and St Werburgh 1461-1899, St John 1620-1885 and St Michael 1665-1872, in *Some Irish lists*, vol. 3 **[IR/G 125]**. Apprentices to surgeons on the staff of Meath Hospital, Dublin, 1775-1887, in *Some Irish lists*, vol. 3 **[IR/G 125]**

Santry: *History & description of Santry & Cloghran parishes, county Dublin*, by B.W. Adams (London, 1883) **[IR/L 146]**

Taney: *The parish of Taney, a history of Dundrum, near Dublin*, by F.E. Ball & E. Hamilton (1895) **[IR/L 78]**. Church wardens of Taney, in *Some Irish lists*, vol. 3 **[IR/G 125]**

MONUMENTAL INSCRIPTIONS

Abbotstown: burial ground, in *Irish genealogist*, vol. 6, no. 6 (1985) 824-7 **[IR/PER]**

Baldoyle: **[Enquiry Desk, Shelf 9]**

Blackrock: Dean's Grange cemetery **[MF ...]**

Chapelizod: church and churchyard, in *Irish genealogist*, vol. 5, no. 4 (1977) 496-505 **[IR/PER]**

Clonsilla: churchyard, in *Irish genealogist*, vol. 6, no. 5 (1984) 680-4 **[IR/PER]**

Coolock: **[Enquiry Desk, Shelf 9]**

Crumlin: St Mary's Church, in *Irish genealogist*, vol. 7, no. 3 (1988) **[IR/PER]**

Dalkey: church and churchyard, in *Irish genealogist*, vol. 5, no. 2 (1975) 250-4 **[IR/PER]**

Dublin: Ballybough Jewish Cemetery, in *The Jews of Ireland*, by L. Hyman (1972) 267-272 **[JR/GEN]**; in Christ Church Cathedral (1878) in *Some Irish lists*, vol. 6 **[IR/G 128]**; Deans Grange Cemetery **[MF 701]**; Bully's Acre & Royal Hospital, Kilmainham **[Enquiry Desk, Shelf 9]**; Merrion Row, Huguenot Cemetery **[IR/M 26]**; St Andrew coffin plates, in *Irish genealogist*, vol. 5, no. 1 (1974) 131-9 **[IR/PER]**; St Catherine's Church & Churchyard **[Enquiry Desk, Shelf 9]**; St Michael & St John coffin plates, in *Irish genealogist*, vol. 5, no. 3 (1976) 368-9 **[IR/PER]**. *See also Directory of graveyards in the Dublin area: and index and guide to burial records* (Dublin Public Libraries, 1988) **[IR/L 160]**

Esker: churchyard, in *Irish genealogist*, vol. 6, no. 1 (1980) 54-58 **[IR/PER]**

Glasnevin: Prospect Cemetery, extracts, in *Louisiana genealogical register*, vol. 22, no. 3 (1975) 265-75 **[US/PER]**

Irishtown: St Michael's Church of Ireland, in *Irish genealogist*, vol. 7, no. 4 (1989) **[IR/PER]**

Kilbarrack: **[Enquiry Desk, Shelf 9]**

Kilbride: churchyard, in *Irish genealogist*, vol. 6, no. 3 (1982) 378-381 **[IR/PER]**

Killiney: Old churchyard, in *Irish genealogist*, vol. 4, no. 6 (1973) 647-8 **[IR/PER]**

Kilmactalway: churchyard, in *Irish genealogist*, vol. 6, no. 3 (1982) 380 **[IR/PER]**

Kilmahuddrick: churchyard, in *Irish genealogist*, vol. 6, no. 3 (1982) 381 **[IR/PER]**

Kilmainham: Bully's Acre & Royal Hospital graveyards **[Enquiry Desk, Shelf 9]**

Leixlip: churchyard, in *Irish genealogist*, vol. 4, no. 2 (1969) 110-l6 **[IR/PER]**

Loughtown Lower: churchyard, in *Irish genealogist*, vol. 6, no. 3 (1982) 380-1 **[IR/PER]**

Lucan: church and churchyard, in *Irish genealogist*, vol. 5, no. 6 (1979) 763-7 **[IR/PER]**

Monkstown: church, in *St John's, Monkstown* by R.W. Harden (1911) 68-9, 87 **[IR/L 69]**; churchyard, in *Irish genealogist*, vol. 4, no. 3 (1970) 201-12, and no. 4 (1971) 349-62

[IR/PER]
Newcastle: church and churchyard, in *Irish genealogist*, vol. 6, no. 2 (1981) 219-26
[IR/PER]
Palmerstown: church and churchyard, in *Irish genealogist*, vol. 5, no. 5 (1978) 650-3
[IR/PER]
Raheny: [Enquiry Desk, Shelf 9]
Rathcoole: church and churchyard, in *Irish genealogist*, vol. 6, no. 4 (1983) 523-5 **[IR/PER]**
Rathfarnham: in *Irish genealogist*, vol. 7 (1986-9) 293-306 **[IR/PER]**
Taney: church and churchyard, in *The parish of Taney: a history of Dundrum, near Dublin, and its neighbourhood* by F.E. Ball & E. Hamilton (1895) 27-52, 63-4 **[IR/L 78]**

NEWSPAPERS

various: extracts (mostly about clergy) from Dublin newspapers *[Pue's Occurrences, The Dublin Gazette, Falkiner's Dublin Journal, &c]*, in *Some Irish lists*, vol. 5 **[IR/G 127]**; 2nd and 3rd series, vol. 6 **[IR/G 128]**
Pilot, Dublin, 24 November 1828 to 16 February 1849 **[MF 2540-61]**
Wilson's Dublin Magazine: marriage and obituary notices 1762-3, in *Some Irish lists*, vol. 5 **[IR/G 127]**

PARISH REGISTERS

Cloghran: C 1782-1863, M 1738, 1782-83, 1786-1839, B 1732, 1742, 1779-1864 **[IR/R 31]**
Crumlin: St Mary CB 1740-1863, M 1764-1827, 1832-63 **[IR/R 11]** & *Irish memorials association*, vol. 13 **[IR/PER]**
Dalky *see* **Monkstown Union**
Donnybrook: St Mary M 1712-1800, in *Irish memorials association*, vol. 11 **[IR/PER]**
Dublin: St Andrew M 1672-1800 **[IR/R 14]**, M 1801-19, in *Irish memorials association*, vols. 12 & 13 **[IR/PER]**, extracts in *Some Irish lists*, vol. 4 **[IR/G 126]**; St Anne M 1719-1800 **[IR/R 14]**, extracts in *Some Irish lists*, vol. 4 **[IR/G 126]**; St Audoen B 1672-92 index in *Irish memorials association*, vol. 13 **[IR/PER]**, M 1672-1800 **[IR/R 14]**; St Brides C 1633-1714, in *Irish genealogist*, vol. 6 (1980-5) 711 **[IR/PER]**, M 1639-1800 **[IR/R 14]**; St Catherine 1679-1715, M 1715-1800, extracts 1636-78 **[IR/R 15-16]**; St George, extracts from parochial returns, in *Some Irish lists*, vol. 4 **[IR/G 126]**; St John the Evangelist CMB 1619-99 **[IR/R 17]**, M 1700-1800 in *Irish memorials association*, vol. 11 **[IR/PER]**, extracts in *Some Irish lists*, vol. 4 **[IR/G 126]**; St Luke M 1716-1800 **[IR/R 16]**; St Mary M 1697-1800 **[IR/R 16]**, extracts C 1698-1836, extracts M 1813-28, extracts B 1699-1823 in *Some Irish lists*, vol. 6 **[IR/G 128]**; St Michael M 1656-1800 in *Irish memorials association*, vol. 11 **[IR/PER]**; St Michan CMB 1636-1700 **[IR/R 18-19]**, M 1700-1800 in *Irish memorials association*, vol. 11 **[IR/PER]**, B extracts, in *Some Irish lists*, vol. 3 **[IR/G 125]**, extracts 1701-96, in *Some Irish lists*, vol. 6 **[IR/G 128]**; St Nicholas Within M 1671-1800, B 1671-1823 in *Irish memorials association*, vol. 11 **[IR/PER]**, B 1825-63 in *Irish memorials association*, vol. 12 **[IR/PER]**; St Nicholas Without C 1694-1739, M 1699-1738, B 1697-1720 **[IR/R 21]**; St Patrick 1677-1800 **[IR/R 22]**; St Paul B 1702-18 in *Irish memorials association*, vol. 13 **[IR/PER]**, extracts in *Some Irish lists*, vol. 4 **[IR/G 126]**; St Peter & St Kevin 1669-1761 **[IR/R 23]**; St Thomas CM 1750-91, B 1762-91 **[IR/R 27]**, extracts from parochial returns in *Some Irish lists*, vol. 4 **[IR/G 126]**; St Werburgh M 1704-1800 **[IR/R 16]**, extracts in *Some Irish lists*, vol. 4 **[IR/G 126]**; Trinity College 1650-60 **[IR/R 7]**; French Church St Patrick & St Mary C 1668-1818, M 1680-1788, B 1680-1830, in *Huguenot Society*, vol. 7 **[HUG/PER]**; French Church Lucy Lane and Peter Street C 1701-31, M 1702-28, Reconnaissances 1716-30, B 1702-28, 1771-1831, in *Huguenot Society*, vol. 14 **[HUG/PER]**. *See also Directory of graveyards in the Dublin area: and index and guide to burial records* (Dublin Public Libraries, 1988)

[IR/L 160]
Finglas: B 1664-1729 **[IR/R 20]**
Kilgarven: ZC 1811-50, M 1812-1947, B 1819-50, 1878-1960 **[IR/R 34]**
Glasnevin: extracts from parochial returns, in *Some Irish lists*, vol. 4 **[IR/G 126]**
Monkstown Union: 1669-1800 **[IR/R 26]**.
Stillorgan: extracts 1782-1869, in *Some Irish lists*, vol. 4 **[IR/G 126]**

PERIODICALS
Dublin historical record, vols. 1-6 (1938-1944) **[IR/PER]**
Dun Laoghaire Genealogical Society journal, vol. 1, no. 1 (1992) **[IR/PER]**
Gateway to the past: a journal of family history (Ballinteer Branch of Irish Family History Society), vol. 1, nos. 1-5 (1993-5) **[IR/PER]**

SCHOOLS & UNIVERSITIES
Dublin & National University: *Alumni Dublinensis: register of students, graduates, professors and provosts of Trinity College in the University of Dublin 1593-1860*, ed. G.D. Burtchaell and T.U. Sadleir (1935) **[UNI/DUB]**. *Register of names and addresses of past and present members of Trinity College* (1928) **[UNI/DUB]**. *Register of the alumni of Trinity College, Dublin*, ed. K.G. Bailey & H.B. Kennedy (4th edn. 1937) **[UNI/DUB]**. *Register of the alumni of Trinity College, Dublin*, ed. F.W. Pyle (7th edn. 1962) and (8th edn. 1965) **[UNI/DUB]**. *Dublin University Calendar, 1868, 1890* **[UNI/DUB]**. *Of one company: bibliographical studies of famous Trinity men 1591-1951*, ed. D.A. Webb (1951) **[UNI/DUB]**. *An annual record published by Trinity College, Dublin*: nos. 1 (1949), 2 (1950), 11 (1959), 18 (1966), 19 (1967), 20 (1970) **[UNI/Tracts]**. *National University of Ireland Calendar 1918, 1939, 1944* **[UNI/IRE]**. *University College, Dublin Calendar 1936-7* **[UNI/IRE]**
Dublin: *Gladly learn and gladly teach: a history of Alexandra College and School, Dublin, 1866-1966*, by A.V. O'Connor & S.M. Parkes (c.1972) **[SCH/ALE]**. *One hundred years of Mountmellick School: history of the school, with proceedings of the 1886 Centenary and a complete list of scholars (1786-1886)* (1886) **[Apply to staff]**
Rathfarnham: *St Columba's College, Rathfarnham: register from 1843 to 1926*, ed. Wardens Rice & Whelan **[SCH/DUB]**; *Roll of Honour 1914-1918* **[SCH/DUB]**; *Columban* (various) **[SCH/Tracts]**
Rathmines: *Rathmines School: the school roll from the beginning of the school in 1858 until its close in 1899*, ed. T.F. Figgis & T.W.E. Drury (1932) **[SCH/RAT]**

FERMANAGH

CENSUSES
County: *The 1901 Irish census index, vol. 1, county Fermanagh*, by L.K. Meehan (Fort McMurray, Microfiche, 1994) **[Shelf 12]**

LISTS AND DIRECTORIES
1824 *Pigot & Co's Directory*, extract for Irvinestown/Lowtherstown, in *North Irish roots*, vol. 3, no. 2 **[IR/PER]**
1880 *County Fermanagh one hundred years ago: a guide and directory 1880*, by H.N. Lowe (Belfast, 1990) **[IR/D 18]**

LOCAL HISTORY
Maps: Ordnance Survey Maps: *Belleek, Pettigo & N.W. Fermanagh 1900* (reprinted 1990) **[M 473]**; *Derrygonnelly & District 1899* (reprinted 1991) **[M 543]**; *Enniskillen: three town plans 1905* (reprinted 1987) **[M 225]**; *Lisnaskea, Newton Butler and the Upper*

Erne 1900 (reprinted 1989) **[M 356]**; *Tempo & Maguiresbridge 1900* (reprinted 1990) **[M 435]**

County: *Griffith's Valuation* index and copy of co. Fermanagh (Mfc, 1986) **[Apply to staff]**. *Ordnance Survey Memoirs of Ireland*, ed. A. Day, P. McWilliams, &c.; vol. 4, Parishes of County Fermanagh I 1834-5: Enniskillen & Upper Lough Erne (Belfast & Dublin, 1990) **[IR/L 106]**; vol. 14, Fermanagh II 1834-5: Lower Lough Erne (1992) **[IR/L 116]**

Crom Castle: *Crom Castle: an account of some plantation castles on the estate of the Earl of Erne*, by the Earl of Erne (n.d.) **[Ireland Tracts 1]**

Enniskillen: *Enniskillen parish and town*, by W.H. Dundas (Dundalk, 1913) **[IR/L 44]**

MONUMENTAL INSCRIPTIONS

Enniskillen: church and churchyard, in *Enniskillen parish and town* by W.H. Dundas (1913) 42-4, 91-119 **[IR/L 44]**

PARISH REGISTERS

Enniskillen: CB 1673-1772 extracts **[Box 86, Folder 11]**
Lisknaskea: 1804-15 index **[IR/R 30]**.

GALWAY

LISTS AND DIRECTORIES

1834 List of inhabitants (extracts) in united parishes of Kinvarra, Duras and Killina, in *Galway roots,* vol. 2 **[IR/PER]**

LOCAL HISTORY

Galway: *The Compossicion Booke of Conought 1585*, ed. A.M. Freeman (Irish Manuscripts Commission, 1936) and *Index*, ed. G.A. Hayes-McCoy (1942) **[IR/L 21-22]**. *Books of survey and distribution, being abstracts of various surveys and instruments of title 1636-1703; vol. 3, County of Galway*, ed. B.M. Choille (Dublin, 1962) **[IR/L 95; another copy Apply to staff]**. *Galway authors*, by H. Maher (Galway, 1976) **[IR/G 149]**. *A practical handbook to Galway, Connemara, Achill & the west of Ireland* (Dublin, 1900) **[IR/L 46]**

Scarriff: *General valuation of rateable property in Ireland: Union of Scarriff in the counties of Clare and Galway 1855*, (Dublin, 1855) **[IR/L 6]**

MONUMENTAL INSCRIPTIONS

Kilmacduagh: church and churchyard, in *Irish ancestor*, vol. 7, no. 1 (1975) 26-35 **[IR/PER]**

NEWSPAPERS

Galway Mercury & Connaught Weekly Advertiser, January to July and September to December 1846 **[MF 2534]**

PARISH REGISTERS

Abbert: RC M 1821-29 **[IR/M 20]**
Abbey: RC M 1821-29 **[IR/M 20]**
Abbeyknockmoy: RC M 1821-29 **[IR/M 20]**
Adrigool *see* **Liskeave**
Annadown: RC M 1821-29 **[IR/M 20]**
Athenry: RC M 1821-29 **[IR/M 20]**
Ayran: RC M 1821-29 **[IR/M 20]**
Ballynakill: RC M 1821-29 **[IR/M 20]**

Bevonagh: RC M 1821-29 **[IR/M 20]**
Claretuam *see* **Corrofin**
Corrofin & Claretuam: RC M 1821-29 **[IR/M 20]**
Donoghpatrick & Kilcoony: RC M 1821-29 **[IR/M 20]**
Dunmore: RC M 1821-29 **[IR/M 20]**
Garumna: RC M 1821-29 **[IR/M 20]**
Headford: RC M 1821-29 **[IR/M 20]**
Kilbanna *see* **Kilconla**
Kilconla & Kilbanna: RC M 1821-29 **[IR/M 20]**
Kilcoony *see* **Donoghpatrick**
Kilennan: RC M 1821-29 **[IR/M 20]**
Killanan: RC M 1821-29 **[IR/M 20]**
Killererin: RC M 1821-29 **[IR/M 20]**
Lacka: RC M 1821-29 **[IR/M 20]**
Liskeave & Adrigool: RC M 1821-29 **[IR/M 20]**
Moyrus: RC M 1821-29 **[IR/M 20]**
Templetoher: RC M 1821-29 **[IR/M 20]**

PERIODICALS
Galway roots: journal of the Galway Family History Society, vol. 2 (1994) **[IR/PER]**

SCHOOLS & UNIVERSITIES
Galway: *University of Galway Calendar* 1954-5 **[UNI/IRE]**

KERRY

LOCAL HISTORY
County: *Guide to tracing your Kerry ancestors*, by M.H. O'Connor (Glenageary, 1990) **[IR/L
       102]**. *A history of the kingdom of Kerry*, by M.F. Cusack (London, 1871) **[IR/L 48]**.
       *King's history of Kerry, or history of the parishes in the county, with some antiquarian
       notes and queries*, by J. King (Liverpool, 1910) **[IR/L 50]**. *Selections from old Kerry
       records*, by M.A. Hickson (London, 1874) **[IR/L 85]**. *County Kerry past & present: a
       hand-book to local & family history of the county*, by J. King (Dublin, 1931) **[IR/L 47]**;
       also (TS, 1963) **[IR/G 196]**. *A brief account of the rise and progress of the change in
       religious opinion now taking place in Dingle and the west of the county of Kerry,
       Ireland*, by D.P. Thompson (London, 1846) **[IR/L 32]**. *Kerry families; notes*, by
       H.L.L. Denny (Ms not indexed) **[IR/L 49]**. *Newspaper cuttings connected with Kerry*
       collected by Lt.Col. Edward Nash (6 vols. n.d.) **[IR/L 51-6]**
Ardfert: *Ardfert Friary and the Fitzmaurices, Lords of Kerry*, by Miss Hickson (Dublin, 1897)
       [Ireland Tracts 1]
Currow: *Parish priests and curates, Currow Roman Catholic Church 1801-1961*, by A.E.
       Casey (TS, 1963) **[IR/G 196]**
Kenmare: Kenmare estate records, journal No. 2: containing Mr Charles Hume's daily
       receipts of ... Viscount Kenmare's rents 2nd May 1740 to 30th November 1756 &
       Kenmare estate ledger book 1790-1811, by A.E. Casey (TS, 1963) **[IR/G 196]**
Killarney: *Short historical sketches of castles and monasteries in Killarney*, by J.T. Collins &
       J. Quinlan (Killarney, n.d.) **[Ireland Tracts 1]**
Tralee: *The abbey and parish church of Tralee*, by H.L.L. Denny (n.p., 1908) **[Ireland
       Tracts 1]**. *Settlers in Tralee, in the 17th century, with their probable places of origin
       in England*, by H.L.L. Denny (n.p., 1910) **[Ireland Tracts 1]**.

MONUMENTAL INSCRIPTIONS

Aghadoe: churchyard & Protestant cemetery **[IR/G 196]**; *see also* **Fossa**
Aglish: cemetery **[IR/G 196]**
Ardcrone: cemetery **[IR/G 196]**
Barraduff *see* **Glenflesk**
Brosna: church & cemetery **[IR/G 196]**
Castleisland: Protestant church & cemetery **[IR/G 196]**; *see also* **Dysert** and **Kilmurry**
Cordal: cemetery **[IR/G 196]**
Currans: church **[IR/G 196]**
Dysert: cemetery **[IR/G 196]**
Firies *see* **Ardcrone** and **Aglish**
Fossa: church & churchyard **[IR/G 196]**
Glenflesk: cemetery & Barraduff church **[IR/G 196]**
Gneeveguilla: churchyard & cemetery **[IR/G 196]**
Kilbannivane: cemetery **[IR/G 196]**
Kilcummin: cemetery **[IR/G 196]**; *see also* **Rathmore**
Killarney: church and churchyard, in *Miscellanea genealogica et heraldica*, 2nd series, vol. 4 (1892) 60-1 **[PER/MIS]**; Protestant church, cathedral & New RC Cemetery **[IR/G 196]**
Killeentierna: cemetery **[IR/G 196]**; *see also* **Cordal**, **Currans** and **Molahiffe**
Kilmurry: cemetery **[IR/G 196]**
Kilquane: cemetery **[IR/G 196]**
Kilsarcon: cemetery **[IR/G 196]**
Molahiffe: cemetery **[IR/G 196]**
Muckross Abbey: abbey, graveyard & cemetery **[IR/G 196]**
Nohovaldaly *see* **Gneeveguilla**
Rathmore: churchyard, Old Chapel cemetery & RC **[IR/G 196]**; *see also* **Kilquane**

NEWSPAPERS

Kerry Evening Post: all births, marriages & deaths reported 1824-64, by B.M. & D.B. O'Connell (TS, 1963) **[IR/G 196]**

PARISH REGISTERS

Aghadoe *see* **Killarney**
Ballincusland *see* **Castleisland**
Blennerville: M 1830-33 **[IR/R 31]**
Castleisland: RC (includes Cordal & Scartaglen in parishes of Castleisland & Ballincuslane) C 1823-72 **[IR/G 196]**
Castlemaine: Presbyterian M 1853-9 (with Births 1868-94, Marriages 1857-1912, and Deaths 1858-1949 from local newspapers) **[IR/R 31]**
Cordal *see* **Castleisland**
Currens *see* **Currow**
Currow: RC (civil parishes of Killeentierna & Currens) C 1808-23, 1871-1900, M 1803-1900, parish priests & curates 1801-1961 **[IR/G 196]**
Kilgarvan: C 1811-50, M 1812-1947, B 1819-50, 1878-1960 **[IR/R 34]**
Kilgobbin: M 1713-51 **[IR/R 31]**
Killarney & Aghadoe: RC C 1810-33 **[IR/G 196]**
Killeentierna *see* **Currow**
Scartaglen *see* **Castleisland**
Tralee: M 1796-1817 **[IR/R 31]**.

PERIODICALS
Kerry archaeological magazine, vols. 1-4 (1908-1918) **[IR/PER]**
Kerry magazine, ed. F.C. Panormo, vols. 1-3 (1854-1856) **[IR/PER]**

KILDARE

LISTS AND DIRECTORIES
1788 *Lucas's General directory of the kingdom of Ireland*, extracts for Athy, in *Irish provincial directories* **[IR/D 1]**; also in *Irish genealogist*, vol. 3, no 10 (1965) **[IR/PER]**

LOCAL HISTORY
County: *The Civil Survey 1654-1656; vol. 8, County of Kildare*, by R.C. Simington (Dublin, 1952) **[IR/G 22]**
Ballitore: *An Irish genealogical source: the roll of the Quaker School at Ballitore county Kildare*, by E.J. McAuliffe (Dublin, 1984) **[IR/L 88]**
Celbridge: *General valuation of rateable property in Ireland: Barony of Ikeathy and Oughterany, Union of Celbridge, 1850* (Dublin, 1850) **[IR/L 3]**. *Griffith's valuation of county Kildare: that part of the Barony of South Salt which is included in the Union of Celbridge, 1850*, by R. Griffith **[IR/L 157]**

PARISH REGISTERS
Naas: extracts 1679-1852, in *Some Irish lists*, vol. 4 **[IR/G 126]**

PERIODICALS
Journal of the Co. Kildare Archaeological Society, January & July 1913, July 1914, January 1915, July 1924 **[IR/PER]**

SCHOOLS
Ballitore: *An Irish genealogical source: the roll of the Quaker School, Ballitore*, by E.J. McAuliffe **[IR/L 88]**
Naas: *Clongowes Wood College: school list 1814-1932* **[SCH/CLO]**. *The Congownian*, vol. 18, no. 1 (1947) **[SCH/CLO]**

KILKENNY

CENSUSES
Aglish and Portnascully: 1821, in *Irish ancestor*, vol. 8 (1976), no. 2 **[IR/PER]**
Aglish: 1841, in *Irish ancestor*, vol. 9 (1977), no. 1 **[IR/PER]**
Aglish: 1851, in *Irish ancestor*, vol. 9 (1977), no. 2 **[IR/PER]**
Iverk: 1821, in *Irish ancestor*, vol. 5 (1973), nos. 3, 4, 5 **[IR/PER]**
Kilkenny, St Patrick's: 1901 **[IR/M 31]**

LISTS AND DIRECTORIES
1788 *Lucas's General directory of the kingdom of Ireland*, extracts for Kilkenny and Thomastown, in *Irish provincial directories* **[IR/D 1]**; also in *Irish genealogist*, vol. 3, no 10 (1965) **[IR/PER]**
1884 *Bassett's Kilkenny city & county guide & directory*, extract for Knocktopher (in *Kilkenny graveyard inscriptions, vol. 1, Knocktopher*) **[Enquiry Desk, Shelf 9]**
1884 *Bassett's Kilkenny city & county guide & directory*, extract for St John's parish, Kilkenny, in *An historical survey of St John's, Kilkenny* **[IR/L 158]**
1906 *Historical sketches of the parishes of Castlecomer, Ballyragget, Connahy, Muckalee and Clogh*, by D. O'Carrell (? 1906) (directory section only) **[IR/D 1906]**

LOCAL HISTORY

Castlecomer: Church wardens of Castlecomer 1799-1847, in *Some Irish lists*, vol. 3 **[IR/G 125]**

Kilkenny County & City: *A guide to genealogical sources in and for Kilkenny city and county published as an aid to family and local research*, by P. Nolan (1995) **[IR/L 170]**. *Knights' Fees in counties Wexford, Carlow and Kilkenny (13th-15th century)*, by E.St.J. Brooks (Irish Manuscripts Commission, 1950) **[IR/L 82]**. *Calendar of Ormond deeds being the medieval documents preserved in Kilkenny Castle*, by E. Curtis, vols. 1 1172-1350, 2 1350-1413, 3 1413-1509, 4 1509-1547, 5 1547-1584 & 6 1584-1603 (Irish Manuscripts Commission, 1933-43) **[IR/G 205-210]**. *Transcripts of Ormond deeds 1603-1715, vols. 1-3: index of persons*, by P. Manning (1995) **[IR/G 211]**. *Genealogical memoirs of the Members of Parliament for the county and city of Kilkenny from the earliest on record to the present time; and for the boroughs of Callan, Thomastown, Inistogue, Gowran, St Canice or Irishtown and Knocktopher from their defranchisement to the Union*, by G.D. Burtchaell (Dublin, 1888) **[IR/L 57]**. Kilkenny School Registers 1685-1800, *see* 'The Eton of Ireland', by T.U. Sadleir in the *Journal of the Royal Society of Antiquaries of Ireland* (vol. 54, 1924) **[IR/PER]**. *An historical survey of St John's Kilkenny: history, people & antiquities*, by J. Doyle (1990) **[includes 1901 census; IR/L 158]**

MONUMENTAL INSCRIPTIONS

Kilbride: burial ground, in *Irish ancestor*, vol. 18, no. 1 (1986) 37-47 **[IR/PER]**

Kilkenny: St John's, 82-93, with St John's Church of Ireland Cemetery, 70-73, with Dunmore Old & New Cemeteries 137-8, and Johnswell Cemetery 160-162, in *An historical survey of St John's Kilkenny: history, people & antiquities*, by J. Doyle (1990) **[IR/L 158]**; St Patrick, graveyard (including 1901 census) **[IR/M 31]**

Knocktopher: graveyard (including Bassett's Directory of Knocktopher 1884) **[Enquiry Desk, Shelf 9, two copies]**

PARISH REGISTERS

Kilkenny, St Mary: extracts, in *Some Irish lists*, vol. 4 **[IR/G 126]**

SCHOOLS

Kilkenny: 'Register of Kilkenny School 1685-1800', by T.U. Sadleir, in *Journal of the Royal Society of Antiquaries of Ireland*, vol. 54 (1924) 55-67 & 152-169 **[IR/PER]**

KING'S COUNTY *see* OFFALY

LEITRIM

LOCAL HISTORY

County: *The Compossicion Booke of Conought 1585*, ed. A.M. Freeman (Irish Manuscripts Commission, 1936) and Index, ed. G.A. Hayes-McCoy (1942) **[IR/L 21-22]**. *County of Leitrim: a roll of all gentlemen who filled the offices of High Sheriff, Sub-Sheriff, Foreman of Grand Jury, Lieutenant of the county, Members of Parliament for the county 1600-1909*, by A. Harrison & J.O. Lawdar (n.d.) **[Box 86 Folder 23]**. *Ordnance Survey Memoirs of Ireland*, vol. 40, Parishes of South Ulster: Cavan, Leitrim, Louth, Monaghan and Sligo, ed. A. Day, P. McWilliams, &c (Belfast & Dublin, 1997) **[IR/L 142]**

Creevelea Abbey: *Creevelea Abbey: official handbook* **[Ireland Tracts 1]**

LEIX or LAOIS *formerly* QUEEN'S COUNTY

LISTS AND DIRECTORIES
1788 *Lucas's General directory of the kingdom of Ireland*, extracts for Mountmellick and
        Portarlington, in *Irish provincial directories* **[IR/D 1]**; also in *Irish genealogist*, vol. 3,
        no. 10 (1965) **[IR/PER]**

LOCAL HISTORY
County: *The history of the Queens County, Ireland together with a history of the septs of
        the county, the O'Mores, O'Dunns, O'Kellys, O'Gormans, O'Lawlors, O'Byrnes,
        O'Dempseys, Fitzpatricks, O'Duffs, O'Brennans, O'Delaneys & MacEvoys and some
        noble families of English extraction*, by D. O'Byrne (1856) **[IR/L 73]**. *History of
        Queens County*, by J. O'Hanlon & E. O'Leary (Dublin, 1907) **[IR/L 93]**
Borris-in-Ossory: *Borris-in-Ossory, Queen's Co.: an Irish parish and its people*, by H.D.
        Walsh (Kilkenny, 1969) **[IR/L 96]**

PARISH REGISTERS
French Church Portarlington: 1694-1816, in *Huguenot Society*, vol. 19 **[HUG/PER]**

LIMERICK

LISTS AND DIRECTORIES
1769 *Directory of Limerick* by John Ferrar (1769; reprinted 1965) **[IR/D 1]**; also in *Irish
        genealogist*, vol. 3, no. 9 (1964) **[IR/PER]**
1788 Lucas's General directory of the kingdom of Ireland, extract for the City of Limerick,
        in *Irish provincial directories* **[IR/D 1]**; also in *Irish genealogist*, vol. 3, no 12 (1967)
        [IR/PER]
1817 City of Limerick Poll Book, in *Irish ancestor*, vol. 17, no. 1 (1985) **[IR/PER]**

LOCAL HISTORY
Limerick County & City: *The history, topography and antiquities of the county and city of
        Limerick*, by P. Fitzgerald and J.J. McGregor (2 vols., Dublin, 1826-27) **[IR/L 61-62]**.
        Limerick: its history and antiquities, ecclesiastical, civil and military, by M. Lenihan
        (Dublin, 1866) **[IR/L 63]**. *Dowd's History of Limerick*, by Rev. James Dowd, 1890,
        ed. C. O'Carroll (Dublin, 1990) **[IR/L 154]**. *Alphabetical list of freemen of the city of
        Limerick 1715-1794* (MS) **[IR/L 91]**. *The Civil Survey 1654-1656: vol. 4, County of
        Limerick*, by R.C. Simington (Dublin, 1938) **[IR/G 18]**. *Story of Limerick*, by R.W.
        Jackson (Dublin & Cork, 1973) **[IR/L 147]**. 'Game licences in co. Limerick 1802-
        1821' in *Irish ancestor*, vol. 16, no. 2 (1984) 98-106 **[IR/PER]**

MONUMENTAL INSCRIPTIONS
Ardcanny: in *Irish ancestor*, vol. 9, no. 1 (1977) 3-5 **[IR/PER]**
Grange: churchyard, in *Irish ancestor*, vol. 10, no. 1 (1980) 49-51 **[IR/PER]**
Kilbehenny: churchyard, in *Irish genealogist*, vol. 2, no. 11 (1954) 349-54 **[IR/PER]**
Nantinan: churchyard, in *Irish ancestor*, vol. 12, nos. 1 & 2 (1980) 53-62 **[IR/PER]**
Rathkeale: Church of Ireland graveyard, in *Irish ancestor*, vol. 14, no. 2 (1982) 105-20; vol.
        16, no. 1 (1984) 53 **[IR/PER]**

PARISH REGISTERS
Marriages of British Service personnel in county Limerick 1698-1842 **[IR/R 25]**
Abington: M 1813-45 index **[IR/R 25]**.
Adare: M 1826-45 index **[IR/R 25]**.

Aney: CMB 1759-1802 index, in *Irish memorials association*, vol. 13 **[IR/PER]** and **[IR/R 25]**
Ardcanny: M 1802-45 index **[IR/R 25]**
Ballingarry: M 1698-1715, 1730-34, 1785-1845 index **[IR/R 25]**
Doon: M 1812-45 index **[IR/R 25]**
Kilfergus: M 1815-45 index **[IR/R 25]**
Kilfinane: M 1804-24, 1831-45 index **[IR/R 25]**
Kilflyn: M 1813-45 index **[IR/R 25]**
Kilkeedy: M 1803-45 index **[IR/R 25]**
Kilmeedy: M 1805-45 index **[IR/R 25]**
Kilscannel: M 1825-45 index **[IR/R 25]**
Limerick: Cathedral (St Mary) M 1726-54, 1759-1845 index **[IR/R 25]**; St John M 1697-1845
index **[IR/R 25]**; St Michael M 1799-1845 index **[IR/R 25]**; St Munchin M 1734-68,
1797-1845 index **[IR/R 25]**; Saint Patrick's M 1700-04 index **[IR/R 25]**
Nantinan: M 1784-1821 extracts, B 1783-1820 extracts **[IR/R 25]**
Rathkeale: M 1744-1845 index **[IR/R 25]**

LONDONDERRY *see* DERRY

LONGFORD

CENSUSES
County: *County Longford and its people: an index to the 1901 census for County Longford*,
by D. Leahy (Glenageary, 1990) **[IR/C 2]**

LOCAL HISTORY
County: *County Longford survivors of the Great Famine: a complete index to Griffith's
Valuation of Co. Longford (1854)*, by D. Leahy (Glenageary, 1996) **[IR/L 174]**.
Griffith's Valuation transcript of co. Longford (Mfc, 1982) **[Apply to staff]**

LOUTH

LISTS AND DIRECTORIES
1715 Borough of Dunleer Poll Book, in *Irish genealogist*, vol. 4, no. 1 (1968) **[IR/PER]**
1968 *Tempest's Annual directory and guide for the town of Dundalk 1968* **[IR/42]**.

LOCAL HISTORY
County: *Ordnance Survey Memoirs of Ireland*, vol. 40, Parishes of South Ulster: Cavan,
Leitrim, Louth, Monaghan and Sligo, ed. A. Day, P. McWilliams, &c (Belfast &
Dublin, 1997) **[IR/L 142]**
Kilsaran Union: *History of Kilsaran union of parishes in the county of Louth being a history
of the parishes of Kilsaran, Gernonstown, Stebannon, Mansfieldtown and Dromiskin*,
by J.B. Leslie (1908) **[IR/L 58]**

MONUMENTAL INSCRIPTIONS
Ardee: churchyard, in *Irish genealogist*, vol. 3, no. 1 (1956) 36-40 **[IR/PER]**
Castlebellingham: church and churchyard, in *History of Kilsaran* by J.B. Leslie (1908) 282-
90 **[IR/L 58]**
Dromiskin: church and churchyard, in *History of Kilsaran* by J.B. Leslie (1908) 304-10 **[IR/L
58]**
Fochart: *Tombstone inscriptions in Fochart graveyard, county Louth*, by D. Maclomhair
(c.1969) **[Ireland Tracts 1]**

Kilsaran: churchyard, RC church and churchyard, in *History of Kilsaran* by J.B. Leslie (1908) 291-9 **[IR/L 58]**

Mansfieldstown: church and churchyard, in *History of Kilsaran* by J.B. Leslie (1908) 311-17 **[IR/L 58]**

Stabannon: church and churchyard, in *History of Kilsaran* by J.B. Leslie (1908) 300-304 **[IR/L 58]**

PARISH REGISTERS

Dromiskin (including **Darver** to 1831): C 1799-1840, M 1805-42, B 1802-1907 **[IR/L 58]**

Kilsaran: C 1818-40, M 1818-1908, B 1818-1908 **[IR/L 58]**

Manfieldstown: C 1825-84, M 1824-45, B 1838-84 **[IR/L 58]**

Stabannon: C 1688-1847, M 1703-1907, B 1699-1907 **[IR/L 58]**

PERIODICALS

County Louth archaeological journal, vol. 6, no. 3 (1927), vol. 7, no. 2 (1930), vol. 8, nos. 2-3 (1934-5), vol. 9, nos. 1, 3-4 (1937-40), vol. 13, no. 5 (1956) **[IR/PER]**

MAYO

LOCAL HISTORY

County: *The Compossicion Booke of Conought 1585*, ed. A.M. Freeman (Irish Manuscripts Commission, 1936) and *Index*, ed. G.A. Hayes-McCoy (1942) **[IR/L 21-22]**. *Full name index to householders: Griffith's, Mayo [1855]*, by A.J. Morris (5 Mfc, 1989) **[Apply to staff]**. *Books or survey and distribution, being abstracts of various surveys and instruments of title 1636-1703; vol. 2, County of Mayo* ed. R.C. Simington (Dublin, 1956) **[IR/G 170]**. *The Strafford inquisition of County Mayo* (Dublin, 1958) **[IR/L 67]**

Ballintubber: *Ballintubber Abbey, co. Mayo: illustrated guide* (Ballintubber, 1967) **[Ireland Tracts 1]**

Clare Island: 'Clare Island survey, Part 3, Place names and family names', by J. MacNeill in *Proceedings of the Royal Irish Academy*, vol. 31 (1931) **[Ireland Tracts 1]**

Newport: *Griffith's Valuation of the Union of Newport, Mayo, 1855*, by R. Griffith **[IR/L 149]**

NEWSPAPERS

Mayo Examiner & West of Ireland Agricultural & Commercial Reporter & Advertiser, 1877-1883 **[MF 2535-7]**

Telegraph or Connaught Ranger, Castlebar, 1836-1838 **[MF 2564]**

PARISH REGISTERS

Achil: RC M 1821-29 **[IR/M 20]**

Aghamore & Knock: RC M 1821-29 **[IR/M 20]**

Annagh: RC M 1821-29 **[IR/M 20]**

Ardnaree: C 1769-1820, B 1700-1823 **[Binding]**.

Aughagowr: RC M 1821-29 **[IR/M 20]**

Balla: RC M 1821-29 **[IR/M 20]**

Balla & Trum: RC M 1821-29 **[IR/M 20]**

Ballinrobe: RC M 1821-29 **[IR/M 20]**

Becan: RC M 1821-29 **[IR/M 20]**

Borriscarra & Robine: RC M 1821-29 **[IR/M 20]**

Burrishole: RC M 1821-29 **[IR/M 20]**

Clare Island: RC M 1821-29 **[IR/M 20]**

Claremorris: RC M 1821-29 **[IR/M 20]**

Crossboyne: RC M 1821-29 **[IR/M 20]**; *see also* **Tagheen & Crossboyne**
Crossmolina: C 1768-77, 1802-3, M 1769, 1775-77, 1802-21, B 1768-77, 1802-21 **[IR/R 31]**
Drum: RC M 1821-29 **[IR/M 20]**
Kilcoleman: RC M 1821-29 **[IR/M 20]**
Kilcommon: RC M 1821-29 **[IR/M 20]**
Kildacomoge *see* **Turlough**
Kilgiver: RC M 1821-29 **[IR/M 20]**
Killala: C 1757-69, M 1759-67, B 1757-98 **[IR/R 31]**
Killmina: RC M 1821-29 **[IR/M 20]**
Kilmoremoy: C 1768-1820, MB 1768-1823 **[IR/R 31]**
Kilvine: RC M 1821-29 **[IR/M 20]**
Knock *see* **Aghamore**
Mayo: RC M 1821-29 **[IR/M 20]**
Nealpark: RC M 1821-29 **[IR/M 20]**
Oughaval: RC M 1821-29 **[IR/M 20]**
Robine *see* **Borriscarra**
Tagheen & Crossboyne: RC M 1821-29 **[IR/M 20]**
Trum *see* **Balla**
Turlough & Kildacomoge: RC M 1821-29 **[IR/M 20]**

MEATH

LISTS AND DIRECTORIES
1831 'A canvas book of the Meath election', in *Irish genealogist*, vol. 7 (1987) 278-88
[IR/PER]

LOCAL HISTORY
County: *Meath ancestors: a guide to sources for tracing your ancestors in co. Meath*, by
N.E. French (1993) **[IR/L 159]**. *The Civil Survey 1654-1656, vol. 5, County of Meath*
ed. R.C. Simington (Dublin, 1940) **[IR/G 19]**. 'High sheriffs of counties Cavan and
Meath 1714-1823', in *Some Irish lists*, vol. 3 **[IR/G 125]**
Kells Union: *General Valuation of Property in Ireland: Union of Kells in the counties of
Meath and Cavan, 1854*, (Dublin, 1854) **[IR/L 4]**
Oldcastle Union: *General valuation of rateable property in Ireland: Union of Oldcastle in the
county of Meath, 1854*, (Dublin, 1854) **[IR/L 5 and IR/L 159]**

MONUMENTAL INSCRIPTIONS
Agher: church and churchyard, in *Irish ancestor*, vol. 10, no. 2 (1978) 129-39 **[IR/PER]**
Athboy: church and churchyard, in *Irish ancestor*, vol. 13, no. 1 (1981) 52-63, and no. 2
(1981) 113-24 **[IR/PER]**
Balsoon: churchyard, in *Irish ancestor*, vol. 8, no. 2 (1976) 94-6 **[IR/PER]**
Clady: church and churchyard, in *Irish ancestor*, vol. 16, no. 1 (1984) 9-13 **[IR/PER]**
Drumlargan: churchyard, in *Irish ancestor*, vol. 12, nos. 1 & 2 (1980) 82-3 **[IR/PER]**
Duleek: churchyard and Old church, in *Irish genealogist*, vol. 3, no. 12 (1967) 538-40
[IR/PER]
Dunboyne: church & graveyard, in *Irish ancestor*, vol. 11, no. 1 (1979) 54-68, and no. 2
(1979) 137-53 **[IR/PER]**
Kells: churchyard extracts, in *Irish genealogist*, vol. 3, no. 11 (1966) 439-44 **[IR/PER]**
Killaconnigan: graveyard, in *Irish ancestor*, vol. 16, no. 2 (1984) 107-117 **[IR/PER]**
Loughcrew: church and churchyard, in *Irish ancestor*, vol. 9, no. 2 (1977) 85-101 **[IR/PER]**
Moy: churchyard, in *Irish ancestor*, vol. 6, no. 2 (1974) 85-96 **[IR/PER]**

Moyagher: churchyard, in *Irish ancestor*, vol. 8, no. 1 (1976) 9-12 **[IR/PER]**
Oldcastle: churchyard 'Monumental inscriptions of Oldcastle, county Meath' by R. ffolliott & H.E. Jones in *Riocht na Midhe* (c.1967) **[Ireland Tracts 1]**
Rathmore: church and churchyard, in *Irish ancestor*, vol. 7, no. 2 (1975) 70-82 **[IR/PER]**

MONAGHAN

LOCAL HISTORY
Maps: Ordnance Survey Maps: *Clones & Roslea 1907* (reprinted 1994) **[M 754]**; *Monaghan 1907* (reprinted 1995) **[M 786]**
County: *Ordnance Survey Memoirs of Ireland*, vol. 40, Parishes of South Ulster: Cavan, Leitrim, Louth, Monaghan and Sligo, ed. A. Day, P. McWilliams, &c (Belfast & Dublin, 1997) **[IR/L 142]**
Clones: *Griffith's Valuation of the Union of Clones (part of) ... in the county of Monaghan, 1861*, by R. Griffith **[IR/L 155]**

NEWSPAPERS
Northern Standard & Monaghan, Cavan & Armagh Advertiser, 1842-1844 **[MF 2538]**
Northern Standard & Monaghan, Cavan & Tyrone Advertiser, 1885 **[MF 2539]**

OFFALY *formerly* KING'S COUNTY

LOCAL HISTORY
Maps: Ordnance Survey Maps: *Banagher 1909* (reprinted 1995) **[M 507]**; *Birr 1909* (reprinted 1995) **[M]**; *Tullamore 1910* (reprinted 1996) **[M]**

MONUMENTAL INSCRIPTIONS
Killaderry: graveyard **[Enquiry Desk, Shelf 9]**
Daingean: **[Enquiry Desk, Shelf 9]**
Offaly: **[Enquiry Desk, Shelf 9]**

QUEEN'S COUNTY *see* LEIX or LAOIS

ROSCOMMON

LOCAL HISTORY
Maps: Ordnance Survey Maps: *Athlone (East) [Roscommon & Westmeath] 1912* (reprinted 1995) **[M 798]**
Roscommon: *The Compossicion Booke of Conought 1585*, ed. A.M. Freeman (Irish Manuscripts Commission, 1936) and *Index*, ed. G.A. Hayes-McCoy (1942) **[IR/L 21-22]**. *Books of survey and distribution, being abstracts of various surveys and instruments of title 1636-1703; vol. 1, County of Roscommon* ed. R.C. Simington (Dublin, 1949) **[IR/L 94; another copy Apply to staff]**. *Freeholders of County Roscommon 1768-1799*, by P. Manning (TS, 1987) **[IR/L 99]**. *The great Irish famine: words and images from the Famine Museum, Strokestown Park, County Roscommon*, by S.J. Campbell (1994) **[IR/G 215]**

MONUMENTAL INSCRIPTIONS
Cloonakille: graveyard, in *Moylfinne journal*, vol. 4, no. 4 (1997) 1-4 **[IR/PER]**

NEWSPAPERS

Roscommon Reporter, 3 January 1857 to 12 March 1859 and 6 to 27 October 1860 **[MF 2562]**

Roscommon Weekly Messenger, 5 January to 21 December 1850 **[MF 2563]**

PARISH REGISTERS

Kiltullagh: RC M 1821-29 **[IR/M 20]**

PERIODICALS

Moylfinne journal, vol. 4, no. 3 (Sep. 1997), to date **[IR/PER]**

SLIGO

LOCAL HISTORY

County: *The Compossicion Booke of Conought 1585*, ed. A.M. Freeman (Irish Manuscripts Commission, 1936) and *Index*, ed. G.A. Hayes-McCoy (1942) **[IR/L 21-22]**. *General valuation of Ireland: county Sligo 1843* **[IR/L 75]**. *Ordnance Survey Memoirs of Ireland*, vol. 40, Parishes of South Ulster: Cavan, Leitrim, Louth, Monaghan and Sligo, ed. A. Day, P. McWilliams, &c (Belfast & Dublin, 1997) **[IR/L 142]**

Sligo: 'Seventeenth century hearth money rolls with full transcript relating to county Sligo', by E. MacLysaght, in *Analecta Hibernica*, No. 24 (Irish Manuscripts Commission, 1967) **[IR/L 76]**. *General valuation of Ireland: county of Sligo, 1843* **[IR/L 75]**

PARISH REGISTERS

Castle Connor: C 1867-72, B 1867-73 **[IR/R 31]**

TIPPERARY

CENSUSES

Shanrahan & Tullagherton: Census of Protestants, 1864-70 [in *Irish ancestor*, vol. 16, no. 2 (1984), 61-7] **[IR/PER]**

LISTS AND DIRECTORIES

1788 *Lucas's General directory of the kingdom of Ireland*, extracts for Burrisoleigh, Carrick-on-Suir, Cashel, Clonmel, Nenagh, Thurles and Tipperary, in *Irish provincial directories* **[IR/D 1]**; also in *Irish genealogist*, vol. 3, no. 11 (1966) **[IR/PER]**

LOCAL HISTORY

County: *Tipperary's families: being the Hearth Money records for 1665-67*, ed. T. Laffan (1911) **[IR/L 161]**. *The Civil Survey 1654-1656, vol. 2, County of Tipperary: Western and Northern Baronies*, ed. R.C. Simington (Dublin, 1934) **[IR/G 16]**. *The Suir from its source to the sea*, by L.M. McCraith (1912) **[IR/L 77]**

Cashel: 'Mayors of Cashel, 1673-1839', in *Some Irish lists*, vol. 2 **[IR/G 124]**

Fethard: Borough of Fethard rolls of burgesses & freemen 1707-1834, in *Irish genealogist*, vol. 4, nos 2-4 (1969-71) & 6 (1973), and vol. 5, nos. 1-3 (1974-6) **[IR/PER]**

PARISH REGISTERS

Cashel: CMB 1654-57 **[IR/R 7]**

MONUMENTAL INSCRIPTIONS

Kilmore: churchyard, in *Irish genealogist*, vol. 2, no. 10 (1953) 317-21 **[IR/PER]**

Uskane: churchyard, in *Irish genealogist*, vol. 3, no. 2 (1957) 74-5 **[IR/PER]**

NEWSPAPERS
Tipperary Free Press, 1847 **[MF 2565]**
Tipperary Free Press & Clonmel General Advertiser, 1852 **[MF 2566]**

TYRONE

CENSUSES
County: *The 1901 Irish census index, vol. 2, county Tyrone* by L.K. Meehan (Mfc, Fort McMurray, 1996) **[Apply to staff, Shelf 12]**

LISTS AND DIRECTORIES
1824 *Pigot & Co's Directory*, extract for Omagh, in *North Irish roots*, vol. 2, no. 8 (1991) **[IR/PER]**
1839 *Kinders' New directory for the City of Londonderry ...*, extract for Strabane, in *North Irish roots*, vol. 2, no. 2 (1990) **[IR/PER]**
1879 Strabane polling list, in *British Columbia genealogist,* vol. 15, no. 2 **[CAN/BC/PER]**

LOCAL HISTORY
Maps: Ordnance Survey Maps: *Augher, Clogher, Aughnacloy 1902* (reprinted 1991) **[M 507]**; *Castlederg & Newtownstewart 1900* (reprinted 1992) **[M 619]**; *Irvinestown, Fintona & Dromore 1908* (reprinted 1990) **[M 556]**; *Omagh 1906* (reprinted 1994) **[M 784]**
County: *The Civil Survey 1654-1656, vol. 3, Counties of Tyrone, Donegal & Londonderry*, by R.C. Simington (Dublin, 1937) **[IR/G 17]**. *Ordnance Survey Memoirs of Ireland*, ed. A. Day, P. McWilliams, &c.; vol. 5, Parishes of County Tyrone I 1821, 1823, 1831-6: North, West & South Tyrone (Belfast & Dublin, 1990) **[IR/L 107]**; vol. 20, Tyrone II 1825, 1833-5, 1840: Mid & East Tyrone (1993) **[IR/L 122]**
Aghalow: *Vestry records of the church of St John, Parish of Aghalow, Caledon, co. Tyrone, 1691-1807*, by J.J. Marshall (Dungannon, 1935) **[IR/L 7]**
Castle Caulfield: *History of St Michael's Church, Castle Caulfield (parish of Donaghmore)*, by Y.A. Burges (Dungannon, 1936) **[Ireland Tracts 1]**

MONUMENTAL INSCRIPTIONS
Castle Caulfield: church, in *History of St Michael's church, Castle Caulfield (Parish of Donaghmore)* by Y.A. Burges (1936) 8-10 **[Ireland Tracts 1]**
Clogher: Cathedral graveyard, in *Clogher Cathedral Graveyard* by J.I.D. Johnston (1972) **[IR/M 16]**
Lambeg: churchyard **[Ireland Tracts 1]**

PARISH REGISTERS
Arboe: C 1775-1813, 1824-71, M 1773-1808, 1824-45, B 1776-1813, 1824-1906 **[IR/R 28]**
Ballyclog: 1826-89 extracts **[IR/R 31]**
Castlecaulfield St Michael: C 1746-1870, M 1741-1882, B 1741-1870 **[IR/R 8-9]**
Clonoe: C 1825-59 extracts, M 1819-42 extracts, B 1826-50 extracts **[IR/R 31]**
Donaghenry: C 1733-1845 extracts, M 1735-1842 extracts, B 1733-59 & 1811-38 extracts **[IR/R 31]**
Drumglass: 1677-1849 extracts **[IR/R 31]**
Killyman: C 1747-1837 extracts, M 1783-1860 extracts, B 1755-1844 extracts **[IR/R 31]**
Kilskeery: C 1767-1835, 1837-44 extracts, M 1778-1841, B 1796-1841 **[IR/R 30]**
Tullanisken: 1804-73 extracts **[IR/R 31]**

WATERFORD

CENSUSES
City of Waterford, 1821, extracts only, in *Irish genealogist*, vol. 4, nos. 1 & 2 (1968-9) **[IR/PER]**

LISTS AND DIRECTORIES
1788   *Lucas's General directory of the kingdom of Ireland*, extracts for Dangarvan, Passage East and City of Waterford, in *Irish provincial directories* **[IR/D 1]**; also in *Irish genealogist*, vol. 3, no. 10 (1965) **[IR/PER]**
1807   'How Waterford city voted in 1807', in *Irish ancestor*, vol. 8 (1976) 18-32 **[IR/PER]**
1839   City of Waterford register of electors, in *Irish genealogist*, vol. 8, no. 2 (1991) **[IR/PER]**
1894   *Egan's History, guide and directory of county and city of Waterford*, by P.M. Egan (1894) **[IR/D 3]**

LOCAL HISTORY
County: *Griffith's Valuation* index and copy of co. Waterford (Mfc, 1987) **[Apply to staff]**. High sheriffs of co. Waterford 1270-1891, in *Some Irish lists*, vol. 2 **[IR/G 124]**. *The feuds of the Bishops of Waterford and Lismore* (n.d.) **[IR/G 51]**. *The French settlers in Ireland: the settlements in Waterford*, by T. Gimlette (Waterford, 1856) **[IR/G 51]**. *The Suir from its source to the sea*, by L.M. McCraith (1912) **[IR/L 77]**

Waterford: *Council books of the corporation of Waterford 1662-1700, together with new documents of 1580-82*, ed. S. Pender (Irish Manuscripts Commission, 1964) **[IR/L 80]**. City of Waterford roll of freemen 1542-1650, in *Irish genealogist*, vol. 5, no. 5 (1978) 560-72 **[IR/PER]**. Mayors of Waterford 1324-1891, in *Some Irish lists*, vol. 2 **[IR/G 124]**. Bailiffs & sheriffs of Waterford city 1522-1891, in *Some Irish lists*, vol. 3 **[IR/G 125]**. *Old Waterford, its history and antiquities: a lecture*, by R. Atkins (Waterford, 1894) **[Ireland Tracts 1]**. *Annals of the Danish church of St Olaf's (The ancient Cathedral of Waterford)*, by T. Gimlette (n.d.) **[IR/G 51]**. *The Dominican Priory of Saint Saviour, Waterford* (n.d.) **[IR/G 51]**

MONUMENTAL INSCRIPTIONS
Affane: in *Irish genealogist*, vol. 2, no. 9 (1952) 285-9 **[IR/PER]**
Clashmore: churchyard, in *Irish genealogist*, vol. 2, no. 8 (1950) 246-9 **[IR/PER]**
Whitechurch: churchyard, in *Irish ancestor*, vol. 5, no. 1 (1973) 28-33 **[IR/PER]**

PARISH REGISTERS
Dunmore, East: (Crook, Faithlegg, Kill St Nicholas, Rathmoylan) 1730-1864 **[IR/R 30]**
Lismore: Cathedral M 1692-1767, 1773, 1784-1869, in *Irish genealogist*, vol. 6 (1980-5) 38-47, 247-51 **[IR/PER]**
Waterford: Cathedral C 1655-57, M 1698-1706, in *Irish genealogist*, vol. 6 (1980-5) 276-84, 685; Presbyterian C 1770-1813, M 1761-1802, in *Irish ancestor*, vol. 13 (1981) **[IR/PER]**; photocopy **[IR/R 30]**

SCHOOLS
Waterford: *Newtown School List of Scholars 1798-1891* (1892) **[SCH/NEW]**. *Newtown School Centenary (1798-1898): history of the school, lists of old and new scholars, etc.* (1898) **[MF 1830 and SCH/NEW]**

WESTMEATH

LISTS & DIRECTORIES
1832 County Westmeath register of electors, in *Irish genealogist*, vols. 5 (1974-9) 235-49 & 772-89, and 6 (1980-5) 77-98 **[IR/PER]**

LOCAL HISTORY
Maps: Ordnance Survey Maps: *Athlone (East) 1912* (reprinted 1995) **[M 798]**; *Athlone (West) 1912* (reprinted 1995) **[M 799]**; *Mullingar 1911* (reprinted 1996) **[M]**

MONUMENTAL INSCRIPTIONS
Ballyloughloe (Mount Temple): churchyard, in *Irish ancestor*, vol. 2, no. 2 (1972) 105-12 **[IR/PER]**.
Delvin: St Mary's Churchyard, in *Irish ancestor*, vol. 14, no. 1 (1982) 39-57 **[IR/PER]**

PARISH REGISTERS
Killucan: 1700-75 **[IR/R 24]**.
Rathconnell: extracts 1797-1861, in *Some Irish lists*, vol. 4 **[IR/G 126]**

WEXFORD

CENSUSES
Marshallstown: 1867, in *Irish genealogist*, vol. 6 (1980-5), 652-69 **[IR/PER]**

LISTS & DIRECTORIES
1776 Borough of Wexford roll of freemen, in *Irish genealogist*, vol. 5 (1974-9) 103-21, 314-34, 448-63 **[IR/PER]**
1788 *Lucas's General directory of the kingdom of Ireland*, extracts for Enniscorthy, Gorey, New Ross, Taghmon and Wexford, in *Irish provincial directories* **[IR/D 1]**; also in *Irish genealogist*, vol. 3, no. 10 (1965) **[IR/PER]**
1885 *Wexford county guide & directory 1885* (reprint by G.H. Bassett, 1991) **[IR/D 1885]**

LOCAL HISTORY
County: *The Civil Survey 1654-56, vol. 9, County of Wexford*, by R.C. Simington (Dublin, 1953) **[IR/G 23]**. *History of county Wexford to 1877*, by G. Griffiths (n.d.; ? incomplete) **[IR/L 81]**. *Knights' Fees in counties Wexford, Carlow and Kilkenny (13th-15th century) with commentary*, by E.St.J. Brooks (Irish Manuscripts Commission, 1950) **[IR/L 82]**
New Ross: Borough of New Ross roll of burgesses 1658-1839, in *Journal of Proceedings of Royal Society of Antiquaries of Ireland*, vol. 21 (1892) 298 **[IR/PER]**. 'Sovereigns (mayors) of New Ross, co. Wexford before 1875', in *Some Irish lists*, vol. 2 **[IR/G 124]**

NEWSPAPERS
Wexford Independent, 1881, 4 January to 9 December 1882, 3 January to 8 August 1883, 1884-1896 **[MF 2569-84]**

PARISH REGISTERS
Coolanick/Oylegate/Enniscorthy: RC Z 1854-1930, M 1908-30, D 1876-1931 **[IR/R 34]**

WICKLOW

LISTS AND DIRECTORIES
1788 *Lucas's General directory of the kingdom of Ireland*, extracts for Arklow, Bray and Wicklow, in *Irish provincial directories* **[IR/D 1]**; also in *Irish genealogist*, vol. 3, no. 10 (1965) **[IR/PER]**

LOCAL HISTORY
Maps: Ordnance Survey Maps: *Holywood 1931* (reprinted 1987) **[M 257]**
County: *Full name index to householders: Griffith's, Wicklow [1852-4]*, by A.J. Morris (Mfc, 1989) **[Apply to staff]**

MONUMENTAL INSCRIPTIONS
Glendalough: Cathedral churchyard, in *Irish genealogist*, vol. 2, no. 3 (1945) 88-93 **[IR/PER]**

SCHOOLS
Bray: Aravon School: *The Aravonian and school register 1862-1962*, ed. J.R.B. Studdert **[SCH/ARA]**